SHOWING MASTERCLASS

Allister Hood and Burroughprince at the Horse of the Year Show (Anthony Reynolds LBIPP, LMPA)

LEARN WITH THE EXPERTS

SHOWING MASTERCLASS

• with Allister Hood and Wendy King

VANESSA BRITTON

David & Charles

To Elizabeth Polling :
a true inspiration to the showing scene

ACKNOWLEDGEMENTS

My very grateful thanks go first and foremost to the stars of the show: Allister and Anne Hood and Wendy King, without whom this book would not have been half as much fun to write. When writing a book such as this which follows a particular discipline, there is a danger that only the positive sides of the sport are presented. I must therefore congratulate them all on being so honest about a sport out of which they derive both their living and their pleasure. I am aware that I must have asked some pretty stupid questions at times, and at others touched on areas where it just isn't 'polite' to ask such things. However, they took it all in their stride, with undeniable enthusiasm and good humour, and because of such an open attitude I have managed to produce my aim: a book that doesn't just 'paper over the cracks' but is an honest portrayal of the current showing scene.

Secondly, I am indebted to Kate Ames, editor of *Australian Horse and Rider* magazine, for her unfailing enthusiasm in sending the Australian commentary and in co-ordinating all the Australian contacts, especially during the last few weeks of writing when faxes were flying backwards and forwards through the night. As a result of her efforts I have learned a great deal about the Australian showing scene, and although I know we have only skimmed the surface I feel the richer for it.

Last but by no means least, I am thankful to all those at the top of the sport who provided many anecdotes relating to their own showing careers. Again, honesty was the key, and only those comments which came 'straight from the heart' have been used. These people are: Vin Toulson; Robert Oliver; John and Sue Rawding; Moggy and Sally Hennessy; Betty Powell; Gerald Evans; the Walker family (especially Maureen) and Caroline Wagner – for often 'having the last word', I thank them all.

VANESSA BRITTON

All photographs by the author unless otherwise credited
Line illustrations by Eva Melhuish

A DAVID & CHARLES BOOK

Copyright © Vanessa Britton 1996
First published 1996

Vanessa Britton has asserted her right to be identified as author of this work in accordance with the Copyright, Designs and Patents Act 1988.

A catalogue record for this book is available from the British Library.

ISBN 0 7153 0310 4

Printed in England by BPC Paulton Books Ltd
for David & Charles
Brunel House   Newton Abbot   Devon

CONTENTS

WHAT IS SHOWING?

One of the most fascinating things about showing, and the one which can lead to either frustration or elation on the part of exhibitors and spectators alike, is that so much depends upon opinions. And whether you are competitor or spectator, showing becomes addictive. Thus when the judge's decision reflects your own choices, you can become quite excited, especially if you happen to be standing at the top of the line; but when the judge's opinions and tendencies differ greatly with yours you may be quite baffled. However, you can learn a great deal from watching both the judge and the competitors in the ring, and if you attend many shows and watch complete classes, you soon begin to develop an 'eye for a horse', that elusive quality which makes judges 'judges', and spectators 'would-be' judges.

Showing is quite unlike any other equestrian discipline, as one judge's opinion may differ completely from another's regarding the same horse, making it quite unlike racing where it is the first past the post, or showjumping where it is the one who jumps a clear round in the fastest time who wins. It is true that a really top class horse will hold its position of supremacy with most judges; but horses are not machines, they have their off-days and behave unexpectedly. Couple this with a situation where 'new stars' are always emerging, and you begin to see that a champion's ruling position can never be considered permanent.

It is very easy to accept being the winner in a show class, but far more difficult to be a good loser. However, if you choose showing as your 'sport' then the first thing you need to accept is that you should not go into the show ring unless you are prepared to submit yourself and your horse to the judge's opinion, as at the end of the day his or her decision is final.

One of the nice things about the activity of showing is that absolutely anyone can participate with any horse. If your horse cannot jump or do dressage, or you cannot jump, then you can always show him and there is a lot of fun to be had as long as you show at a level that suits you. Being placed at a local village show with a native ridden pony that you have brought straight off the moorlands and trained yourself, will, I assure you, give you just as much pleasure as that which a top professional gets from winning at Wembley on a horse that has been primed for the event all year.

Showing is an activity that you must want to do for pleasure because the expenses far outweigh any prize money – you will have lost money before you go out of the yard. Those who make it to the top will often get up in the small hours of the morning to travel, and then exercise their horse for a class later that day; and if they are actually lucky enough to win (which very few are), they may take home a cash prize equivalent to one or two sets of horse-shoes. It is the thrill of winning that counts – anyone may win occasionally, but the goal is to win consistently, or at least always to come near the top. However, you cannot hope to win or be placed unless you have mastered the art of 'ringcraft', and this is something that can only be learned by experience; you must therefore be prepared for a long, but nevertheless enjoyable learning expedition.

Showing is a sport dictated by the seasons, and so this book will take you on a guided tour from winter through to autumn, unravelling a unique and fascinating portrait of work behind the scenes and of skilful showmanship as it goes…

Brown Sabre, ridden by Cathryn Scott, was always a consistent winner and
with such a horse you just keep going; she retired sound to stud at the end of the 1994 season
(Anthony Reynolds)

1

WHAT MAKES A SHOW HORSE?

ACQUIRING THE SHOW HORSE

The best time to acquire a show horse is undoubtedly during the winter months. This will give you time to prepare your new horse for the ring, undertaking all the essential tasks of creating a rapport with him, also establishing a fitness programme, and looking after trimming and presentation. However, horses do not always appear at their best through the winter, so you do need to know what to look for. For the professional showperson it is a case of selecting the most handsome horse, the one that oozes personality – the real 'look at me' type. For the more novice showperson it is not so much a task of selecting the most talented horse, but the one which is most

(Left) Horses do not always look their best through the wintertime as their coats often disguise what is underneath, so you do need to know what to look for (Right) The same horse a couple of months later – would you have been able to visualize a horse such as this underneath?

suitable: the best horse in the world is useless if its owner cannot ride it. The idea is to enjoy what you are doing, and in order to do so, you need to select a horse that is going to suit your own character, commitment to the game, and your finances. There is a great difference between buying a first horse, and buying a first 'show' horse; a common mistake is to buy an animal that is too good for your current experience and ability, so be careful not to 'over-horse' yourself in your quest for success.

In order to buy the right sort of horse it is always a good idea to enlist the help of professionals, people such as Allister Hood and Wendy King who have been showing for years and have had to learn, to their cost, through their own mistakes. It does not take too many times of buying something unsuitable to start acquiring the knowledge of what sort of horse is right for what sort of job. Taking a professional with you when viewing potential purchases will help you to avoid such costly mistakes, and will ensure you end up with a horse that is right for you.

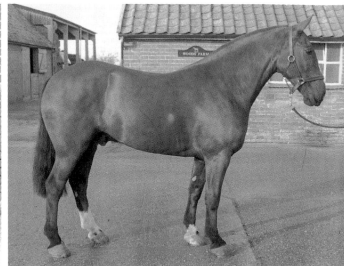

To breed or to buy a potential show horse?

It may seem that trying to breed a show horse is a good option, especially if you have your own mare with good conformation and a placid temperament. However, both Allister and Wendy are of the opinion that it is always better to *buy* a show horse if you can, rather than trying to breed one, as then you can be more selective. If you breed a foal you are going to be stuck with the result, which might be far less than ideal. There are no guarantees when

To try and breed a show horse is to take a gamble; but if you want to breed anyway and are lucky enough to breed a good one, then any successes are all the sweeter

breeding a horse; you can use a mare and a stallion which both have excellent conformation, and still end up with something that is put together completely wrong. It is certainly not a cheaper option either, so although you might be lucky and get a really nice horse, why leave it to chance?

• A BREEDER'S VIEW •

Professional stud owner and show producer Sue Rawding really does not mind whether she buys or breeds a good show horse: in her opinion the main thing is to acquire the right one, by whatever means. 'Obviously it is a bit special to do well on something you have bred,' she says, 'but it is better to do well with something you have bought, than to do terribly with something you have bred. Really good horses are so few and far between that you have to acquire them when you see them in any way you can. For instance, I would love to have a small hunter, but we have never found one or bred one yet that we have rated highly enough. We think we might have just found one, but he is only two years old at present, so we have just got to wait and see if he makes the grade.

'It was a very great thrill to win the Roy Creber In-Hand Championship at Wembley with Little Patch as a two-year-old,' says Sue. 'We bred him out of a Thoroughbred mare called Madame Constance from the Party Politics line, and his sire was Funny Man.'

'Realistic was the best horse we have ever bred,' says husband John Rawding. 'If you could guarantee to breed horses like that every time, there would be no need to buy one. Unfortunately we lost him at five years old due to a twisted gut that could not be operated on, so we will never know just how far he could have gone; but he was a saint of a horse – every time he went out into a show ring his whole attitude said "I'm here!"'

If you are lucky you might end up with something nice, and then being successful with something you have bred is a bit special

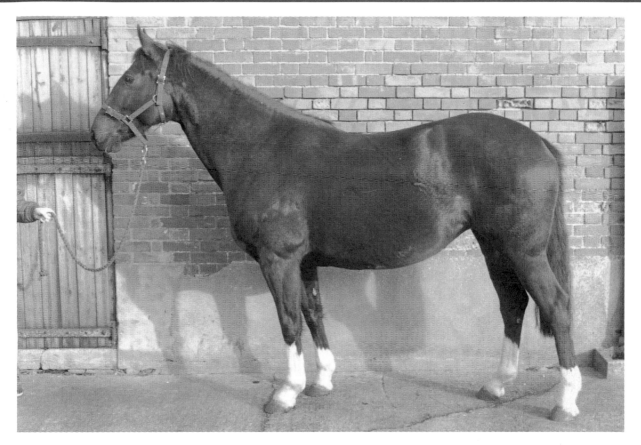

*(Above) A horse 'bred' for showing. However, it is long
in the body and short and upright in the neck, so will
never go very far in the ring*
*(Right) In an ideal world most people would prefer to
show something they had brought on themselves, but it
is not always possible*

Showing from scratch, or buying a proven show horse?

In an ideal world most people would prefer to show
young horses that they have backed and trained
themselves, but not everyone has the experience or
time to make a success of it. Says Wendy:

'I do prefer showing new prospects, as then any
successes are of my own doing. It is not such an
achievement to go out and win on a horse that has
been produced by someone else, and perhaps won
lots of times before. Youngsters have not got into
any bad habits, either; but of course they are hard
work, and you can never be sure that they are going
to turn out as you hope. Older, more experienced
horses are fine for people new to showing as they
will help to provide the necessary experience, but

It doesn't take much knowledge to realize that this horse has pretty poor conformation. If Wendy had gone to look at this horse with a view to showing, she would not take the assessment any further

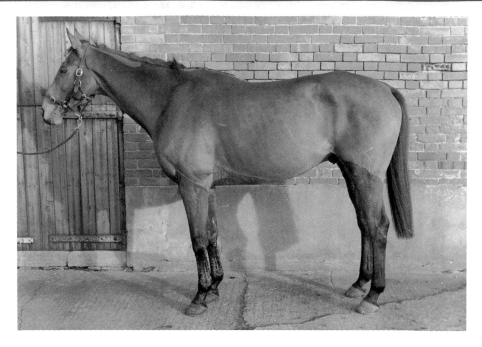

they must not have become sick of the job, as then they become a bit "ring-crafty" and may try it on with their new, and less experienced rider. An older horse that has done a different job but is still a nice type may be the ideal for someone new to showing; or perhaps a horse that has done just one season, so that he knows his job but has not become too ring-crafty. However, there is no reason why an experienced rider who is simply new to the sport of showing, should not produce a young horse for the ring.'

• ANNE STURGES' VIEW •

To buy or breed a show horse? The old saying 'Fools breed them for wise men to buy' is still so true. One feels tremendous satisfaction in breeding your own, certainly, but it is not worth it commercially. Added to this is the time aspect – as I'm getting older time goes so fast, but even I don't want to have to wait four to six years and be leading it around with my zimmer frame! I feel, therefore, that I would recommend buying unless you know exactly what your mare will produce from a known stallion and have time to wait for it to mature. An unknown mare and unknown stallion could produce anything; at least if you buy you can see what you are getting.

Some do's and don'ts when buying

The first thing Wendy does when looking at a potential show horse is to take a look at its limbs and conformation: if one or other of these are not basically good, she does not go any further with the assessment. However, if she likes the type and it is clean, she will then see it trot up and down; and providing she still likes what she sees, she will ask to see it ridden. While under saddle she will look at its way of going, 'its movement and action' when ridden. As she generally buys young horses she is not looking for perfection, but is looking to see if an animal is basically a good mover; if it is, she knows that such a horse can be worked correctly and improved. Whereas if an older horse does not move well, it is never going to move well!

Having seen a horse ridden, Wendy then experiences its ride for herself. 'You have to feel comfortable on a horse,' she says. 'You want to feel that it has got a good bit of body in front of you, and that you sit into it well. A lot comes down to your own instincts, body shape and personal preferences. I have a rule that if I have any doubts about a horse, I don't buy it, as mistakes are very costly! However, if I have a good feeling about a horse then I will trust my instincts and buy it.'

Allister's buying technique differs from Wendy's in that he would never dismiss anything on the strength of just seeing it in the yard or stable, even

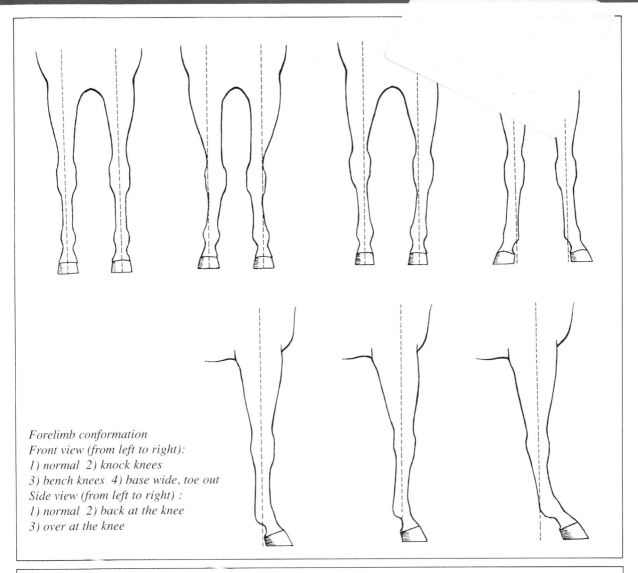

Forelimb conformation
Front view (from left to right):
1) normal 2) knock knees
3) bench knees 4) base wide, toe out
Side view (from left to right) :
1) normal 2) back at the knee
3) over at the knee

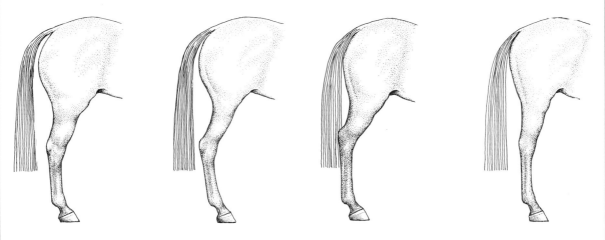

Hindlimb conformation (from left to right) 1) good hind leg 2) sickle hocks
3) hocks in the air d) over-straight hocks

if he only half liked it, but would also see it ridden. He explains:

'There are lots of horses that win classes and which look nothing standing in the yard; but once they are under saddle they can be transformed. If once under saddle I still don't like it, then I would thank the vendor for his time and leave it at that. Should I like what I see, I will then ride the horse. The first thing I evaluate is comfort; I do not want to feel as though I am sitting on a horse's ears – I just want to feel "right" on the horse, and only you can know what feels right for you.

'The next thing to assess is its way of going. You or your adviser should be able to sense whether the horse is going to be difficult, lazy or straightforward to ride, and then you have to decide whether you can actually cope with what you are intending to buy. You may feel that the horse has a lot of potential, but if it is going to be naughtier than you can cope with, then it is not the horse for you; as a combination you will never do well.'

Having the potential show horse vetted is something you should think about seriously

• CHARISMA •

The first thing John Rawding looks for in a horse is presence. 'This is something that if a horse hasn't got you cannot give to him, so it has to be a natural part of his make-up,' he says. 'Obviously the show horse must also have good conformation and movement, and a good temperament is a real bonus.' However, temperament is not the deciding factor for John as he feels you can work at a horse's temperament and forgive him his moods, as long as he has everything else.

For John, the word that sums up the ideal quality for a show horse is 'charisma'.

Vetting

The question of whether to have a horse vetted or not often arises when buying a new horse. On the one hand you want to have the horse vetted because any health problems can be very costly in the long run, or in severe cases may make the horse totally unsuitable for your purpose. On the other hand, however, vetting is expensive and if the horse fails, you then have to find a new horse which is accompanied by another vetting fee and so on. In the end it does all come down to money: if money is not a problem, then always have your horse vetted. Similarly, if you are intending to buy a very expensive horse, always safeguard yourself by making sure it will pass the vet. However, if the horse is not that expensive you might not want to go to the extra cost of having it vetted. In such a situation, if you are not yourself sufficiently knowledgeable to judge whether it is basically sound, always have a more experienced friend look at the horse for you. And even though a show horse might get away with a mild health problem that would fail an eventer, it is unlikely that he will stay a show horse for the rest of his life – so be cautious. Wendy always has the heart and eyes of a potential purchase checked, whatever the horse or its cost. She will go to the expense of having a horse fully vetted if it is costing a lot of money, but will rely on her own judgement for a cheaper horse.

What type of horse have you got?

When looking at a horse with showing in mind, you have to decide whether it fits into a particular showing category or not. There are many horses which are very nice and may be suited to the job of eventing or endurance riding, but which would not fit into any particular showing category. Thus you might find a tall, light-boned horse which would be a lovely hack if it were smaller, but as you cannot make it smaller it is not the horse for anyone with showing ambitions. If you see an advert that says 'lightweight/middleweight', you will know it is

Take a good look at the horse – will it fit into a particular category? This is Face the Music, a small hunter, already clipped as he was needed for the early shows

Regal Max at the beginning of the show season; he is a true lightweight hunter, winning the Royal International and coming third at Wembley in 1994 with Allister. He is owned by Marie Parish and is by Mufrig, out of Regal Zara

The highly successful Brown Sabre. Here we see her having just been brought up at the beginning of the season. She is a very good stamp of large riding horse, by Code Breaker, out of Sheila, owned by the Cooper Corporation and produced by Allister

neither one thing nor the other, and so you should be cautious if looking at it with a view to showing in a particular category, as opposed to a breed. There are some very nice 'in-between' horses, but unfortunately they never do well at showing.

Wendy's ideal show hunter is a lightweight, no less than 16.1hh and no more than 16.2hh. It should have good flat bone, and a depth of bone of at least 8½ inches (21.5cm). Its hind leg should be good with its hocks underneath it and not stuck out behind. 'However, it is extremely hard to find your "ideal" horse,' says Wendy, 'so generally you look for the fewest faults when assessing a horse to buy. If you were to wait for the perfect horse to come along, you would probably still be waiting.'

It is important to decide what type of horse or pony you want to show. The best way of doing this it to spectate at the agricultural shows, as often you find yourself drawn to one particular class; perhaps hunters, or mountain and moorland for instance. Then your task is to find a suitable horse for your chosen category; one that is not only a good sort, but suits your own size and ability as well.

Suitability for the rider

There is no reason why a certain size or type of rider cannot show any type of horse he or she wants except, of course, for side-saddle showing which is confined to lady riders. If you already have a horse and you decide to take up showing, then obviously you will do the best with what you have. However, if you have the opportunity to buy a horse, then it is better to get something that is not over- or under-sized for you. It all comes down to the overall picture and what the judge will see in an imaginary frame around you; so a big heavyweight horse with a small rider will not look as appealing as a larger rider on the same horse: 'The effect is a bit like a pea on drum' says Wendy ' – it just doesn't balance.' Similarly, a small cob is ideal for a small, stocky person, whereas a tall, thin rider

(Top) You do need to have a 'keen' eye when looking at potential show ponies. This is True Mint, a 13hh show hunter pony acquired for Louenna Hood
(Below)This is also a good stamp of show hunter pony, but if you compare it to the one in the previous photo where the pony has just come up from grass, you can see the difference

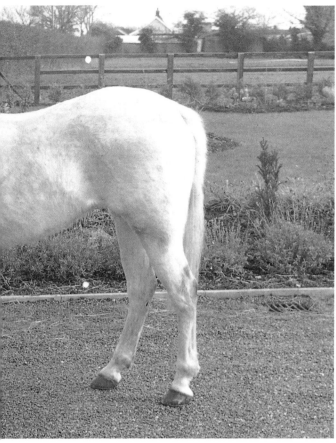

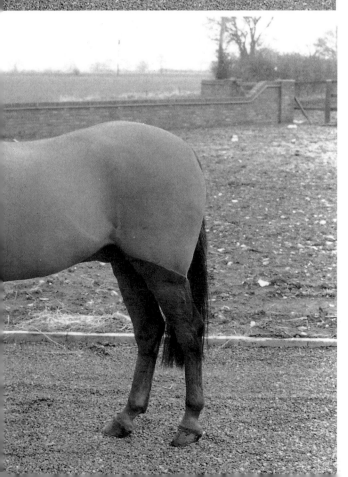

will not present as good a picture on the same horse. Having said that, at the end of the day the judge might evaluate your horse as the best in the ring even if, as its rider, you are not of the 'ideal' size; but you will have to work harder to get the judge to look at you, as his or her first impression will not be an 'eye-opening' one. First impressions are all-important, and you want to be pulled in at the top of the line, rather than be put up from somewhere lower down. More horses win classes from the top of the line, than those that arc put up.

'The horse must also be matched to the rider for the rider to feel at ease,' says Allister. 'As Anne and I often buy horses for other people, we always have to have this in our minds; it is no good buying a potential champion if you know your owner will never get on with it. We might find a horse that is not the best in the world, but if it will suit a particular client and he or she is likely to pick up rosettes on it and have a good time, then he/she is going to have a lot of fun and enjoyment. That is far better than someone owning a fantastic horse that he/she cannot actually ride.'

• ANNE STURGES' BREEDING TIPS •

Why am I successful with my broodmares and foals? I feel strongly that top class mares should always be used. 'Any old mare' sent to a decent stallion is just not good enough. I only breed from tough, sound, good-looking mares who have proved themselves. I like to have their feet X-rayed, and to know that they are capable of producing sound youngstock. I have still got two mares sound and well aged twenty-five and twenty-seven. I also feel that, being a true amateur, I must have the best to be able to compete against the professionals; my standards must be even higher than theirs. It is slightly more open for the amateur in Hunter Brood Mare classes, as the professionals are more inclined to concentrate on the youngstock, but even so you must aim for as near-perfect conformation as possible. Added to this your mare must have that little extra – presence, sparkle or just 'Look at me' – whatever you like to call it.

Old hands or new prospects

Allister believes that a novice person need not go out and buy a 'ready-made' show horse, but nor should he or she buy a young horse that has not seen any life. 'A horse that has hunted, or done a little bit of cross-country or showjumping will have had the rough edges taken off it,' he explains. 'It will be used to going out and about, and will be accustomed to crowds and other horses. Such a horse can then be channelled into being a show horse, and the newcomer can get a lot of satisfaction out of achieving things with it that nobody else has. This is more rewarding than buying a show horse that has already done a lot, when the new owner is only repeating achievements that have already been accomplished by the horse with another rider.'

However, Allister is quick to point out that you should not write off older horses that have been shown with only moderate success before, as many horses do improve with age, and although a horse may not have been particularly successful as a four-year-old, it may come out as a champion at eight. Again, it all comes back to the horse's knowledge, and that is why, in showing terms, a horse can be first today and last tomorrow.

CONFORMATION

A good show prospect should have certain basic qualities, whatever the class. Above all else it should possess that 'sparkle' that will make it stand out in a crowd – the 'charisma', of John Rawding: in a line-up of good horses with equally correct conformation it is this charisma that will separate the winners from the losers. However, this quality is only as good as the horse underneath, and while good conformation can be enhanced by subtle 'tricks of the trade', it cannot be created.

There is something to be said for the term 'beauty is in the eye of the beholder' and this is why judges' opinions vary; but all good judges should recognize certain basic qualities that set the standard for good conformation. And when assessing a horse for purchase, you should be able to distinguish between a horse which might be poor in condition yet still has good conformation, and one which is perhaps very well conditioned but lacks good conformation.

What to look for

- First a horse must be **sound**, with no physical defects that would predispose it to lameness in the future. Be wary of any horse that does not trot up sound without an obvious reason such as a recent injury or swollen leg.
- The **head** should be intelligent, with a broad forehead and a large, kind eye; it should be in proportion to the rest of the body with large, well defined nostrils. The lower teeth should meet the

A horse's head should look intelligent, with a broad face and large, kind eye. This is Melford Cornish Gold (George), Wendy's lightweight hunter (owned by Mr R.D. Coulson)

upper teeth; if they are behind the upper teeth the horse is described as parrot-mouthed, a condition which will put the horse down in the ring. In addition the head should be well set on the neck, with plenty of breathing space between the lower jaw bones near the throat.
- The **neck** should be straight or slightly arched and in proportion in length to the rest of the body; not too thick-set, nor too weak.
- The **shoulder** should be long and sloping from the withers to the point of the shoulder. Such a horse will be a more comfortable ride, as a short,

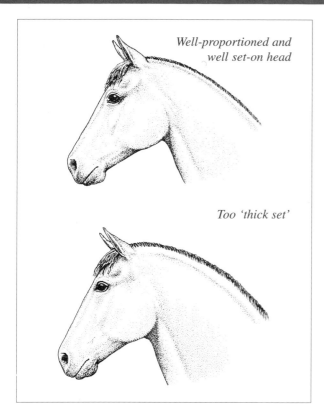

Well-proportioned and well set-on head

Too 'thick set'

joints, and pasterns which are too sloping allow too much strain to be transferred to the suspensory ligaments and tendons.
• The **hooves** should be deep, with adequate room between the heels; narrow, boxy feet can restrict the function of the foot. The frog should be firm and well developed, with a shallow depression in the centre.
• The **hind thighs** should be long, well muscled and well let down, with the second thigh (the gaskin) also strong.
• The **hocks** should be large and fairly square, with the point of the hock well defined.

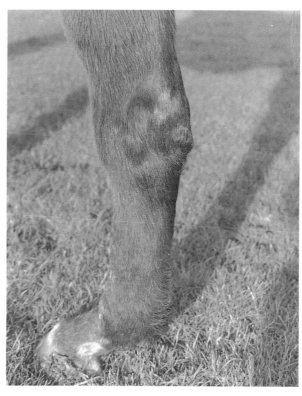

Obviously not the hock of a show horse; this horse would definitely go down the order in the ring

upright shoulder produces a shorter stride.
• The **withers** should be prominent, but not too 'cresty', tapering gently away into the back.
• The **back** should be short and strong, neither dipped nor too wide.
• The **hindquarters** should be straight, strong and broad, reaching well down into the second thigh.
• The **chest** should not be too narrow as this will bring the forelegs closer together, making the horse move too close in front.
• The **girth** should be deep, and the ribs well sprung.
• The **forearm** should be strong with plenty of muscle.
• The **knees** need to be broad and flat to take the weight of the body, with the bone of the forearm and the cannon bone in a straight line, with an evenly placed knee.
• The **cannon** should be strong and short with clearly defined tendons behind. The amount of 'bone' a horse is said to have refers in fact to the measurement of the whole lower limb region just below the knee.
• The **pasterns** should be sloping and set at a gentle angle. Upright pasterns are not effective in preventing the buffering of concussion on the

Naturally there must be some scope for variation in the above points, depending on the type of horse, and accounting for the fact that the perfect horse is a rare animal indeed. Nonetheless, a good show horse will posses most of these attributes. Certain breeds can vary considerably in conformation, so what might not be ideal in the hunter may be perfectly acceptable in a pure-bred horse of a certain breed. (See Chapter 9 for more information on specific breeds.)

Always look at the horse's way of going loose in the field if you can; a horse with good conformation is also likely to have a good action

When viewing a potential purchase ask to have him trotted up, before you ever ride him

Action

A horse with good conformation is also likely to have good action; however, action does vary between breeds of horses. For example, hacks or hunters should move fairly close to the ground with a long, free and easy stride, whereas a native pony such as a Welsh pony will have more knee action, and a gaited horse such as a hackney or an American Saddlebred will have a high knee action. Paces should be straight, active and rhythmic, with equal stride lengths. It is always a good idea to watch a horse loose in the field, as he will then be able to show his true paces, uninhibited by handler or rider.

When viewing a horse for purchase ask that he be trotted straight towards you and then past you, taking note of his way of going. Ask yourself these questions: does he move straight? Are his strides free and easy? Does he move in an undesirable fashion, for example does he brush or dish?

Allister and Anne's view on conformation

Allister would not accept a horse with a curb or with very large capped hocks, or anything similar that was very unsightly. 'If these faults are small you can often reduce them with physiotherapy

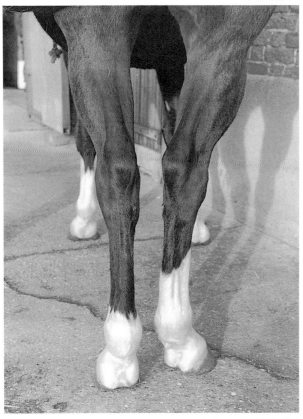

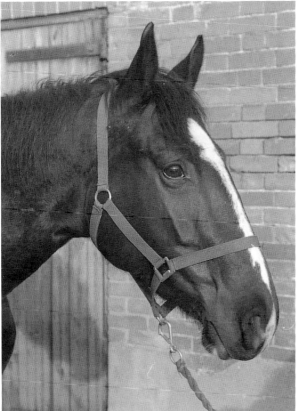

machines,' says Anne, 'so if the horse was otherwise really nice then it would be worth the effort; but the price would, of course, need to be adjusted'. Splints don't worry Allister and Anne very much, as long as they are within reason. Says Allister:

'I do think judges sometimes use splints as an excuse to put a horse down, but if they are looking for such excuses then they were probably going to put the horse down anyway. It would appear that judges simply find it easier to give you a reason for your horse being put down, rather than just saying, "Well, I'm sorry, but I liked those horses above you better". You also ought to avoid very bad, or oddly shaped feet, as good feet are important in show horses.

'A good head is fairly important, but this does depend on the category of the horse – obviously a hack has got to have a "prettier" head than a hunter, which can have a more "workmanlike" head. It also depends on the horse's personality. Even a horse with a plain head can look something providing it has a nice large eye, always has its ears forwards, and has that certain presence, or charisma. A horse can have the prettiest head in the world, but if it goes with its eyes looking backwards all the time and its ears flat back, then it is never going to look anything; so always notice how the horse carries his head when he is being worked.

'You can select appropriate tack to complement individual horses' heads, but basically the horse has got to say "look at me" underneath. When a horse puts his head over the stable door it has got to appeal to you *personally* if you are going to enjoy owning and competing him.

'As far as colour goes, I don't really have any particular preference, and I feel the same about white markings. A good horse is a good horse despite its colour or markings – although I do feel that a grey can often get away with a multitude of sins, in a way that a similar horse of another colour would not.'

(Top) 'Cow hocks' are another weakness, undesirable in the show horse. There is nothing you can do to improve such a conformational defect

(Below) Even a horse with a plain head can look something, providing it has a nice large eye and its ears are always forwards. A broad double bridle will improve this horse's head enormously

• ANNE STURGES' IDEAL HORSE •

I think the most important thing in my ideal horse (or pony) is temperament. He must be willing and happy to do anything I ask of him in whatever sphere he is going to compete. Having been a Pony Club DC and Riding Club Chairman for many years, I have seen so many keen children and middle-aged ladies lavishing their time, love and money on difficult, ungenerous and downright horrid horses and ponies. Oh for the well adjusted horse or pony who is happy to do his best for you!

• VIN TOULSON'S IDEAL HORSE •

'The ideal show horse must have the right temperament and should immediately catch the eye when it enters the ring. It must have a quality head, which along with its neck is well set on. A good sloping shoulder with plenty in front of the saddle is essential. It should be deep-bodied and short-backed (neither hollow- nor roach-backed) and be should be well "ribbed up". It must have a good foreleg – not badly over or back at the knee – and must have really good bone below the knee. Its pasterns should not be too sloping or too straight, and a well shaped foot is essential. The same applies to the hind leg, although there should not be too great an angle at the hock. A good show horse will also have a good tail carriage and it should, of course, be free from any visible unsoundness or serious blemish.

'All show horses and ponies must move straight, and not turn a toe in or out, or dish. The hunter and hunter pony should have a low, free action that covers the ground at all paces. The hack and show riding horse or pony must be able to shorten the stride to that of a hack canter, whereas Welsh Cobs will be expected to have a lot of knee action.'

Wendy's view

Wendy would not accept a horse with curbs either, or any other sign of weak hocks, as she considers this to be a very bad fault in a show horse (or for any other discipline, for that matter). 'A horse with something as obvious as a bowed tendon, or a sway or roach back would also be out,' she says, 'although splints are not necessarily a factor that would turn me off a horse, especially if they were small. However, when it comes to conformation you must have an "eye for a horse"; a horse might have good basic conformation, but where poor schooling has developed the muscles incorrectly, it can look awful. But I can look at a horse and know whether I can rectify something like that, and so turn the horse back into one with a nice outline.

'When assessing a horse for showing you need to evaluate its "permanent" conformation – the musculoskeletal structure – and its "developed" conformation: that which a trainer or rider produces by working the horse correctly, or incorrectly, as the case may be.'

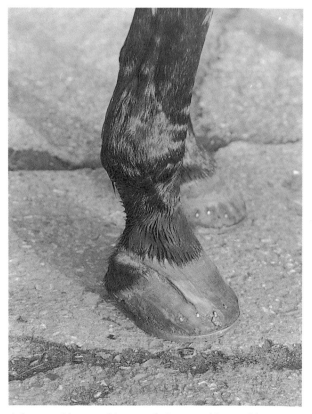

A horse with something as obvious as this would certainly be put down in the show ring

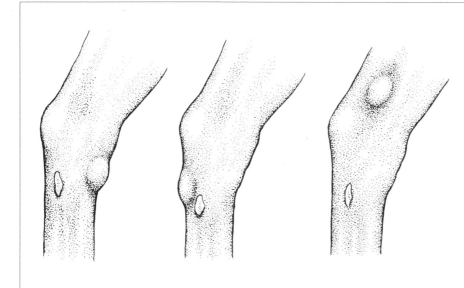

Any sign of weak hocks is a bad fault. Faults of the hock (from left to right): Bone spavin; Curb; Thoroughpin

Wendy also feels that a nice head is very important. 'Unless everything else about a horse was really nice, a plain head would put me off,' she says. 'However, a really good horse with a plain head can be helped by a carefully chosen and fitted bridle – and of course the type of horse comes into it; a hunter can get away with a much plainer head than a hack, for instance.'

FAULTS AND VICES

Vices can often be annoying, but do they affect a horse in the show ring? Wendy would not buy a crib-biter or wind-sucker, because she feels it is difficult to keep the weight on them. Additionally she feels that such abnormal behaviour may be to the detriment of other youngsters in the yard, because they may copy. She says:

'As long as the horse was well conditioned, such vices would not affect a show horse in the ring, although personally, I find horses that crib-bite or wind-suck extremely irritating when I am working in the yard. However, if you are prepared to allow for such vices there is no reason why you should not buy an afflicted horse for showing – but do consider its condition carefully; how a horse copes with a vice problem really does depend on the individual. Thus those which have developed such vices because they are anxious types are often hard to keep in good condition, whereas other horses

Vices such as crib-biting are often enough to put people off buying a horse; however, if a really lovely animal is considered to be a winner, any vice it has becomes rather less important

• WEAVERS •

John Rawding hates a weaver, even to the point that if it were a really good horse he still wouldn't buy it. 'It also depends if it's a mare or not,' says wife Sue, 'as vices such as crib-biting, weaving and wind-sucking you wouldn't want passed down. And, of course, you do also have to think about a re-sale value. However, good horses come in all sorts of packages, and if it's a winner, well then that's more important than any vice.'

seem to show no ill-effects. It is a matter of choice, however; and always bear in mind that such a vice should be reflected in the price – and similarly, when and if you come to sell the horse, he will not fetch as high a price as a vice-free animal of comparable quality, even if he has won quite a lot in the show ring. Ideally you don't buy a horse that has got any vices, but if you see a really lovely horse and know it is a winner, the fact that it has got a vice becomes rather less important.'

There are no vices that would put Allister off buying a horse for showing, unless he were simply buying it from a dealer's point of view to sell on. 'In fact,' he explains, 'virtually all our best horses have been crib-biters, and they had developed the habit long before they came to us, so we bought them in full knowledge of the vices. To be quite honest I couldn't care if a horse lies on its back, puts its legs in the air or walks on the roof,' says Allister, 'as long as when it comes out of its stable it does its job and the problem doesn't affect its looks in any way. Also pony people are far more prejudiced against such vices than horse people, even to the extent that these habits will stop them from buying what is otherwise the perfect pony.'

2

FEEDING AND WINTER MANAGEMENT

BASIC FEEDING PRINCIPLES

While Wendy's horses are turned away they receive oats, carrots and hay. When they are brought in depends on the weather, though ideally this would be just after Christmas so that they don't lose any condition out in the field. The feeding routine then changes and they will have barley, bran and nuts added to the diet so they put on condition and muscle. During the period between Christmas and the end of January the horses are in at night but still out in the day; then at the end of January those that are ridden are put into work, although a younger horse which was new to the job would need to start sooner than this. Training also commences for the in-hand horses in order to establish obedience and manners. In all cases the feeding programme is tailored to reflect the work of each horse.

'What we feed depends on what our horses are doing,' says Allister, 'though even if they are turned out and having a rest for three or four months over the winter, they still need to be fed fairly well so that they come back up looking in good condition. This we achieve by feeding plenty of oats and corn. The beginning of the show season is not a time to start trying to put weight on; all you should be doing at this time is turning fat into muscle. While high energy feeds are less desirable for the stabled horse, the horse at grass has plenty of opportunity to let off steam. Once our horses come in, we then begin to reduce these high energy feeds, to ensure a good temperament.'

Wendy checks all her horses twice a day while they are turned away

(Above) At the end of January Wendy's horses are slowly brought back into work
(Right) Getting the horse's weight right takes continual assessment. Here Wendy checks George's weight before any real work commences

Getting the horse's weight right

It is important to be guided by your own horse's condition. Some horses may need more food than you think to keep their weight right, others will need less. It is all a question of observation and constant evaluation, with a weighbridge or a weight-tape if you are not experienced enough to know just by looking.

'Getting the horse's weight right is just a matter of continual assessment,' says Allister, 'and it does help if you can get someone else to help assess your horse's weight; because you see your horse day in, day out, you may not notice the changes, whereas another person will, if he or she hasn't seen the horse for a while.'

There has been a lot of argument about horses

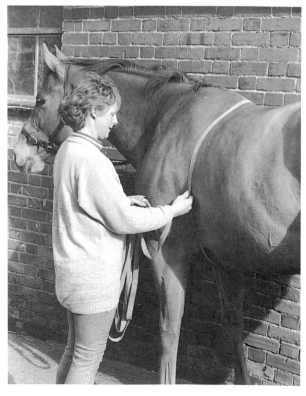

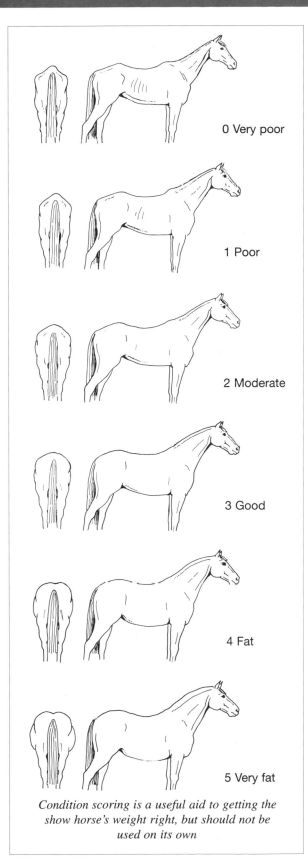

Condition scoring is a useful aid to getting the show horse's weight right, but should not be used on its own

0 Very poor

1 Poor

2 Moderate

3 Good

4 Fat

5 Very fat

being far too overweight in the ring in the UK, especially the in-hand horses. Allister agrees:

'Some of the horses are overweight, but if a horse is worked right, then he shouldn't be; he should be well covered, but his flesh should be muscle, not fat. Undoubtedly it does harm young horses to carry too much weight. One of the problems is that there is so much variation within the weight categories, and people are trying to make their horses appear bigger than perhaps they really are. This is where we need to have more directives from the governing bodies. Basically, a rider weight of 12st 7lb [80kg] for a lightweight is nothing – a strong 14.2 pony or even a lighter 15.2 horse would carry this with ease, so lightweights are obviously up to far more weight than that. If any of the lightweights in the ring were in a dealer's yard as a true hunting type hunter, they would be sold as up to fourteen stone [89kg]. Subsequently, middleweights have become far too big. A real middleweight to my mind would be a good 16.2hh Thoroughbred or near Thoroughbred, with a good bit of limb. All the weights are getting far too big and tall – we seem to have this obsession about breeding big horses, yet at the end of the day you only need a really big horse for a very tall, heavy person. There is a danger that if horses like this continue to be bred they will have little purpose after showing – I mean, how often do you see a big, 17.2hh event horse or showjumper?'

The use of supplements and conditioners

It is well known that if you feed a horse correctly, it will be reflected in a glossy coat. However, it is a mistake to start adding a little bit of this and a little bit of that to a balanced diet, unless you know your horse to be deficient in a certain vitamin or mineral. Wendy feeds cod-liver oil to most of her horses in order to promote good coats. If a particular horse needs to build up a lot of muscle she would use a vitamin E supplement. Or if she has a horse that is a bit highly strung, there are several natural or herbal supplements that she may use to help calm it down (not to be confused with *sedatives*, which are banned).

Allister basically uses straight feeds. 'If something needs a supplement, then we will give it, but we don't give them just for the sake of it as this

Snowline in excellent showing condition. You would not want a young horse to be carrying any more weight than this in the ring

is of no benefit to the horse, and you might as well be throwing your money down the drain.'

BASIC MANAGEMENT

The stabled show horse

One thing you need to consider is the type of stabling you provide for your horse. Too small a stable, and he may be in danger of capping his hocks, or becoming cast. If you have inside stabling you must bear in mind the dust factor – a judge will not be impressed by a horse that coughs all the time – so there must be plenty of ventilation. In addition, contagious diseases will spread far more easily in this type of environment. However, not all horses need to be stabled; in fact the author has won at county shows with horses that have been shown off grass. Generally during the show season most show horses are stabled because it is more convenient and in order to keep their coats fine and smooth. However, whether horses are

• ROBERT OLIVER'S THOUGHTS ON MANAGEMENT •

Good stable management is significant, as successful showing starts at home; unless your horse is well looked after he cannot perform to his best. Discipline when in the stable is also important, and this starts from the moment you open the stable door. Your horse should allow itself to be caught and tied up, and do as it is told when being handled. Discipline which is instilled at home then travels with you into the ring.

*Feeding and bedding also need consideration. A horse must always have a good bed; it doesn't cost any more to give a horse a good deep bed than it does to provide a skimpy bed and keep taking it away from him. Feed in relation to the work your horse is doing and it will show in his coat. However, it is no good buying umpteen additives and the best quality concentrate feed if the **hay** you feed is poor quality. Top quality hay is essential. Show horses are made by paying attention to such details at home.*

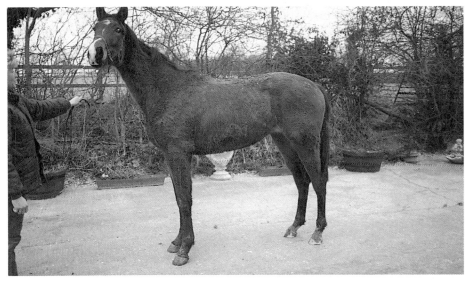

If a horse loses too much condition during the winter it will be hard to put it back on before the show season begins. In this series of photos we see a two-year-old filly sent to Moggy Hennessy at the start of the show season. This photograph was taken when the filly arrived in Moggy's yard in February

Two months later, and the horse has changed beyond all recognition. The only way of achieving this change is through correct feeding and lungeing

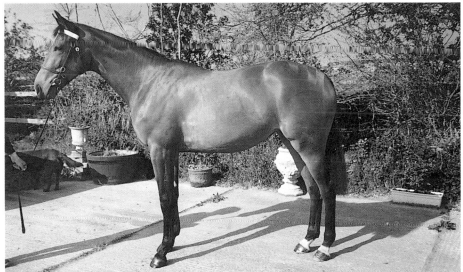

By May the horse had improved so much that she went out and won at the Suffolk County Agricultural show (Anthony Reynolds)

stabled out of the show season depends on the horse's temperament. While Allister does bring all the Thoroughbred horses in at night, he doesn't have a particular policy for stabling all the show horses. 'Some are perfectly happy to be out all the time, others appear to want to come in at night, so we are happy to bring them in,' he says.

Wintering out

If a horse has been turned away after the show season, it will usually be brought back up again just after Christmas. If the weather is particularly bad, however, many people will bring their horses in earlier than this because they don't want them to lose too much condition, as this would be hard to put back on before work was due to start.

• NATURAL MANAGEMENT •

Sue Rawding believes that the only way to produce horses that are going to be happy and do their job well, and which will have a life after showing, is to allow them as natural an existence as possible. All the Rawdings' horses are wintered out without rugs on; they are fed twice a day, and when they do come back in at the beginning of the season they are fresh, in good health and ready to go.

'We always "yard" the foals for their first year,' says John, 'because that is the most important time of their lives. If you don't do your horses well as yearlings, they will not thrive and grow on well.'

Considerations particular to Australia

Australia is a country of extremes in terms of climate, and the climate varies dramatically between cities and states. Accordingly the showing year also alternates, with the northern states holding their major shows during the winter months (when it is still hot) and the southern states holding their show season late or early in the year during mid-summer (see pages 75–81). In Queensland and the Northern Territory, the showing season virtually grinds to a complete halt over the summer months, while the Victorian 'Barastoc' Horse of the Year Show is held in

February, one of the hotter times of the year.

While some areas of New South Wales and Victoria receive snow in winter, this is not common, so the routine of 'wintering' a horse is not practised as a rule. Horses may be 'spelled' (rested) over the winter, although due to some major shows being held in early spring, such as Melbourne Royal, Perth, Hobart, Launceston and Adelaide Royals, many horses are kept in light work throughout the colder months. Winter is, in fact, an extremely active competition time for other equestrian disciplines such as eventing, endurance, showjumping and dressage.

The long-standing drought in New South Wales and Queensland for the past four years has seen feed and transport prices increase dramatically, and accordingly, some members of the show horse community have been forced to curtail their activities; the number of people competing has dropped slightly.

Clipping and rugging

Most UK show horses are turned away during the winter without rugs on, and as a result they grow a naturally long and thick coat. This needs removing before ridden work can be started with the horse, so many show horses will have a clip between Christmas and the end of January. Obviously to compensate for the lack of coat the horse will need rugging, and if he is well rugged this will also encourage a nice smooth summer coat to grow at the appropriate time. With unclipped horses, many people throw on layers of rugs to encourage the horse to lose his winter coat quickly; he may not have a nice summer coat in March, however, as

(Top right) The concept of 'wintering' horses in Australia is not generally practised, as the weather is usually mild. Pure Castle, Australian Champion Galloway in 1993 and 1994. A Thoroughbred mare by Kia Loa, she is extremely elegant and is ridden here by Chris Lawrie (Kate Ames)

(Right) As a result of being turned away during the winter without rugs on, horses will grow a naturally long coat. This is Kingfisher, owned by Mrs Sarah Walker, just after Christmas before his first season showing. He is a five-year-old small riding horse. (Compare this photograph to the one on page 70)

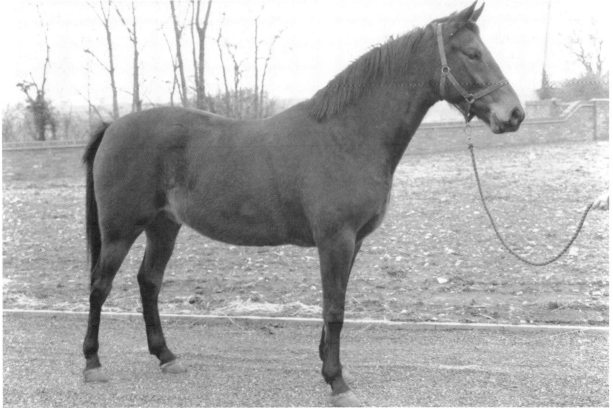

nature will inevitably take its own course – also you must watch that he doesn't become sweaty and uncomfortable, because he will start to lose weight unless the situation is adjusted.

Allister adopts the last policy: once his horses are brought in between Christmas and the New Year, they will be rugged immediately, with three or four rugs to encourage them to moult and to prevent the need for clipping. 'We do try not to clip if we can avoid it,' says Allister. 'Some people also clip horses during the summer if they have grown a summer coat that is not particularly fine,' says Allister, 'but if the horse is healthy, and has been well rugged, this should not be necessary – at least, we have never needed to do it. One exception may be the fairly hairy native ponies that will grow a woolly coat whatever you do.'

• CLIPPING IN AUSTRALIA •

Clipping is a relatively unknown practice in the northern part of Australia, where the heat keeps the horse's coat short throughout the year. It is a regular practice, however, in the southern states.

Variety and protection for the show horse

Many show horses are in danger of being 'over-protected'. It is very important that show horses are allowed to enjoy other activities as well as showing, or they will become totally bored. Of course, people do worry about their top show horse getting injured during such activities, and you do have to be mindful of injuries; but for the sake of the horse, he must have a change of scene. 'I always bear in mind that they are not going to be show horses forever,' says Wendy, 'so they have got to do another job. Many of the horses that have passed through my hands have done everything, including cross country, showjumping and hunting

(Top left) Mr R.D. Colson's Snowline. This filly is produced by Wendy and won the Royal as a yearling in 1993. Here we see her just having been brought up in February for the 1994 season to be shown as a two-year-old hunter

(Left) Four months later and Snowline has been completely transformed

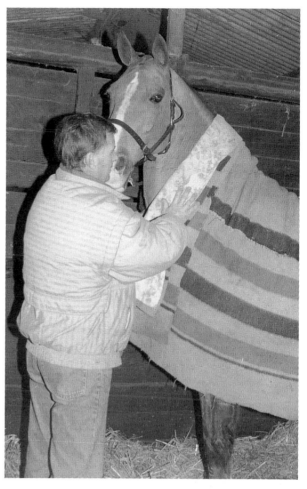

Once Allister's horses are brought in they are rugged immediately to encourage them to moult

as well as showing, and they have had good temperaments and have been perfectly happy. Such horses will keep on showing happily for a lot longer than those which are confined solely to the show ring.'

In order to provide some protection Wendy does turn her show horses out in brushing boots, and most of the time she keeps a rug on them. 'I even keep a light rug on the horses when it is fairly warm,' she says, 'because you don't want the horse to be irritated by flies, and as it has been encouraged to grow a finer coat than it might have done if left without rugs early in the season, it will feel any chills sooner than other horses. Neck covers are a boon, especially with grey horses, as it helps to keep them clean and so saves labour. You can get linen ones for the summer, so the horse need not be uncomfortable.'

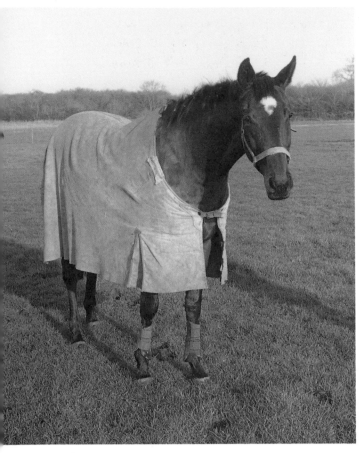

Wendy does turn her show horses out, but in brushing boots in order to provide some protection to the legs

Neck covers are a boon, especially for greys

Safety in the field

In order to prevent injuries Allister never turns his show horses out together. Only one horse will go out at a time, although if a particular individual won't settle on its own then an old, unshod pony is put out with it. Obviously the field must be checked regularly for possible hazards, so that no debris strays into the field unnoticed. You should also watch out for sharp edges on broken fences, and of course barbed wire and other such potentially injurious fencing is just not a risk worth taking for any horse.

It is fairly easy to take all these precautions if you look after your horses yourself, but how do people who work full time in another industry ensure their safety, or top professionals who just haven't enough hands to see to all their own horses personally? One of the answers is that they have a good, reliable team of helpers and staff.

• RECRUITING STAFF •

If you need to employ staff, or haven't the time to look after your own horse(s), it is extremely important to find the right type of person in order that they remain safe and in good health. Moggy and Sally Hennessy have been very fortunate in this respect, as Sally explains:

'We have been very lucky with our staff and we rarely advertise; normally people come to us asking if there are any vacancies. We have rarely taken on anyone we don't already know, normally through friends or by recommendation. When a new "recruit" starts, the most important thing is to get some idea of his or her strengths and weaknesses. Most people have a preference – some like to ride, some prefer to be "on the ground". It is important to have a balance of both kinds of employee in a show yard, and it is up to Moggy as their employer to know who is best at what. To find out, the first thing she does is to put them onto College Jester out on a hack; if they can't get him to go properly, they probably won't stay very long as riders! Next she likes to test out their mane and tail pulling and clipping skills. With so many youngsters about it is very important to be quick, quiet and efficient with all stable management techniques, as show horses have to be trimmed on a weekly basis.'

3

TRAINING AT HOME

FITNESS & EXERCISE

Other than a basic ridden education, you might
think there is little to teach a show horse at home,
as it is surely appearance, rather than ability, which
counts. To a certain extent this is true: obviously a
show horse does not need the technical skill to
perform as does a dressage horse, but nevertheless
it does need to be finely tuned in other ways. As an
example, take the event horse which will almost
always get exited before a competition: it may give
a few bucks and jog about the collecting ring, but
such behaviour is accepted because hopefully it
will perform when asked. In contrast, the show
horse is 'on show' from the minute it enters the
collecting ring until after the lap of honour; should
the judge turn his head and see it misbehaving in
the collecting ring, his first impression will be a
negative one, and the horse will then have to be
pretty special to reverse that judge's opinion once it
is in the ring.

The important qualities of a show horse are:

- good manners
- being responsive to the aids of any rider
- the right attitude
- strong, rhythmic paces
- composure and self-control

The improvement of all these qualities needs to be
considered when devising an exercise and work
régime for the horse. Firstly, however, you need to
ensure that the working environment suits the horse
in order that he may adopt the correct attitude to
learning.

Bringing the Horse up from Grass

The right time to bring a show horse up from grass
is, to a certain extent, a matter of personal choice
and often depends upon individual circumstances.
For example, Allister brings all his horses up from

*Traits such as this certainly need ironing out before you
enter the show ring. While excitable behaviour may be
accepted in the eventer or showjumper, it cannot be
tolerated in the show horse. Here Wendy is having a
sort-out with a recently acquired youngster*

grass at the end of December in order to get an
early start with youngsters and new prospects,
while Wendy may wait until mid- to late January.
This is because Allister has grooms to help with the
everyday care and exercise of the stabled horses,
whereas Wendy has little help and so finds it easier
to wait until her children are back at school, before
bringing her horses in. It is pointless to have your
horse stabled early if you have little time to devote
to him. In such a situation it is more sensible to
wait a few weeks until you know you can commit
enough time and effort to the special needs of a
show horse.

carrying plenty of condition, and this will ensure that he stays in the best of health as his fitness training progresses. Assuming the horse has already been backed, and before any real work starts, a period of long-reining can be very beneficial in building confidence and in getting him to go forwards willingly.

Before any serious ridden education is started, long-reining can be very effective in teaching a young or nervous horse to go forwards willingly

When initially a horse is brought in from a rest period the first things to sort out are his coat and feeding programme. If his winter management and feeding régime have been well catered for (see Chapter 2), he should be in good health and

• HANDLING YOUNGSTERS •

'All our horses are handled regularly as foals,' says John Rawding. 'Then as two-year-olds we nearly always drive them in long reins to get them out and used to being under our control. We may also sit on them every day for a few days, but then they are turned away again. As three- year-olds, we will bring them in for a week during February to sit on them again every day, and then out again. We would pick up again in September, riding them for a month and then turning them out again, until they are brought up as four-year-olds. I don't believe in riding two-year-olds too much, but I do like them to have been sat on and walked and trotted around the school.'

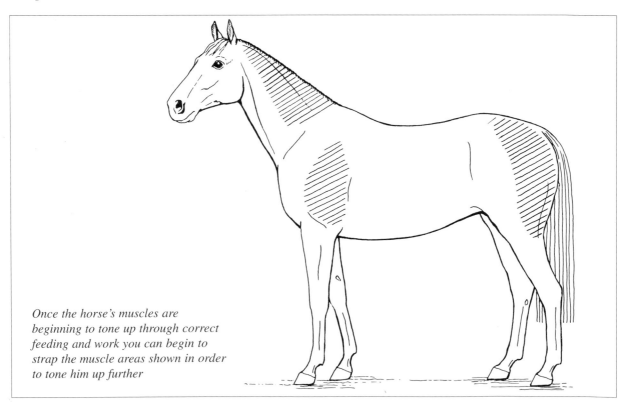

Once the horse's muscles are beginning to tone up through correct feeding and work you can begin to strap the muscle areas shown in order to tone him up further

Implementing a Fitness Programme

Wendy's aim when beginning a horse's exercise routine is to produce an animal that is not fat or flabby, but one whose muscles are toned up. 'This does not mean you want it to be over-fit,' she explains, 'as this would be detrimental to the show horse; you would lose that nice "round" outline, and would also be in danger of it "boiling over" in the ring. You only need it to be fit enough to do the job, but not as fit as an eventer; lots of fast work is not necessary. Conversely if the horse has not had enough work and is just fat, rather than well toned, as soon as you started to travel and show him, the weight would just fall off him.'

At first Wendy walks her horses for about a month, then during the following two weeks introduces some slow trotting. Where a horse is a newcomer to the show ring, light schooling can also commence around this time, although a more experienced horse may not need to begin schooling for another couple of weeks. In Wendy's opinion, the younger horse certainly needs more time spent on it; nevertheless: 'You have to balance the need to get a horse right, against the danger of making him stale before the end of the season, so it is important not to overdo things,' she emphasizes.

Having brought his horses up after Christmas, Allister spends about two weeks walking them around the lanes. 'We don't walk them forever, because this tends to make them too fresh and they would get above themselves,' he explains. Additionally, he feels that the sooner they can get on and do a little work, the more sensible they become, and it also builds them up. 'It's not as if they are racehorses that are going to have extreme pressure put on their legs,' he says, 'and those horses which were shown the previous season wouldn't have had such a long break that they would be totally unfit anyway.'

Planning the Season

While it is true that the younger horse does need more work, he may not be physically or mentally developed enough to cope, so how do you proceed? Firstly you have to have your showing season well planned. Most of the major UK shows are over by July, so you have to decide whether your horse is developed enough to start early, in the hope of

Hamlet, acquired as a new prospect in 1994 by Anne and Allister for Sara Capon. Here he is a six-year-old, and will be shown as a large hack. His sire is Croft Hall, his dam an unnamed Thoroughbred by Dragonara Palace. When this picture was taken he had been in the Hoods' yard for only a few weeks

Allister begins Hamlet's schooling, having already completed a couple of weeks roadwork. At this stage Allister is working on improving suppleness and balance, and establishing a good rhythm (compare this to the picture on page 71 in Chapter 7)

reaching Wembley (US and Australian comparisons are given in Chapter 5), or whether you are going to show him only lightly in his first season, in which case you can start his education a little later and take him to shows later in the year.

If you are aiming a young horse at Wembley it is sensible to plan a break for him mid-season; in Wendy's opinion this would certainly apply to most four-year-olds and often a number of five-year-olds. A good plan is to show the horse until July, then if you have been lucky enough to qualify, to give him a month off before bringing him back up for Wembley. How the horse spends his month off

(Top left) This cob was acquired by Wendy straight from Ireland in August 1994, as a prospect for the 1995 season. A less experienced eye might have passed him by, as in his present state he is not visually appealing and certainly does not look as though he could move well

(Left) Four months later, however, after a lot of hard work on Wendy's part and having been hunted once or twice a week, he is beginning to look like a serious novice prospect for the 1995 season

Some horses naturally stand with that 'look at me' quality. Although this foal's legs are not in quite the right place, the overall picture is a good one; consequently, it will not take long to teach such a horse the correct way of standing

will depend upon his individual character and his mental state. The important thing to bear in mind is that he needs to be kept sweet, so taking him off to do some dressage or a little showjumping may be just as beneficial as an actual rest. However, you also need to consider the physical make-up of the individual horse, and must be careful not to let his showing outline alter due to participation in other activities. Providing you do not overdo things, this is unlikely to be a problem unless the horse becomes especially excited during a particular activity, in which case it may be better to find something else to occupy him. If you simply leave the horse out in the field, then his outline will almost certainly suffer, as will his coat and general appearance, and this may be difficult to restore before the later shows; it is therefore sensible to continue stabling the horse at night.

BASIC IN-HAND EDUCATION
Teaching the Horse to Stand Correctly when In-Hand

A horse that naturally stands correctly when in-hand is a blessing. Ones that do not are at best a challenge, and at worst extremely frustrating. 'It is no good walking a horse out in front of a judge and saying "Well – here he is!"' says Allister.

'As a showman, you have got to present the horse. You have got to tell the judge with your body language and with the horse's body language that this is the best horse he has seen. The horse has got to say, "Look at me, I'm a lot better than you think I am," or "I'm better than all the others!" It is the work you put in at home that will ensure your horse presents himself in this way, and it is even more favourable if it all appears to be smooth and natural. For example Mystic Minstrel has only got to see a camera, and he poses! In a way, no matter how it stands, a truly great horse will *always* look good, but if it also stands up well, then it will look magnificent.'

It can take a considerable length of time to teach a horse to stand correctly; nevertheless most do get the message as long as you persevere and do not lose your temper. The idea is to have all four legs

visible from one side, with those furthest from the judge slightly inside those nearest to him or her (some US breed classes expect a different type of stance, and this is dealt with under each respective heading in Chapter 5). Teaching the horse to stand correctly can be tedious; some take only a few sessions before they get the idea, while others can take weeks, or may never do it without a little fiddling back and forth. However, it cannot be stressed enough that standing a horse up correctly is extremely important, especially if it is to be shown in-hand. Accomplishing this simple act can mean the difference between winning or being placed down the line, as the visual outline is lost if the horse is standing incorrectly.

In order to teach the horse to stand correctly you need to have him in a bridle. First, pick the spot where you are going to ask him to stand, making sure it is level and firm. Walk by his shoulder up to this chosen spot, and without hesitation ask him to stand while stopping decisively yourself. Move around in front of his head, and if his legs are not all showing as described, move him back or forwards a pace until you achieve the desired stance. Once this has been accomplished, praise him well. It is also desirable to have his head up and ears pricked. In order to achieve this you might pick a few strands of grass and wave them at his eye-level to gain his attention, or you could rustle a crisp bag in your pocket, or shake a box of matches. It is important to get your horse used to this at home, as it may cause him to approach you in order to investigate the cause of the noise, or he may back off, both of which he must be restrained from doing.

Standing the horse up correctly can make all the difference to his visual appearance. Here we see a four-year-old just beginning his training with Allister. He is a 15hh show hunter pony, owned by Mrs J. Stewart and Mrs C. Lumsden. The photo on the left shows the difference between the handler's rather negative attitude of saying 'Well, here it is', and (right) presenting the horse to say 'Look at me!'

 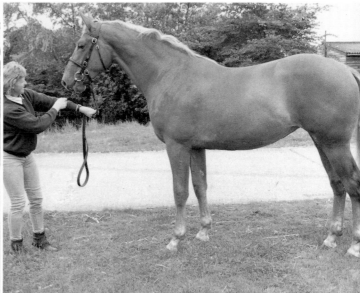

Snowline was a little temperamental as a yearling, so Wendy had to give her a few stern lessons. In the photograph on the left Wendy demonstrates how not to stand a horse in the ring and on the right, the ideal way to stand a horse up. All four legs are visible, the head is up and the ears are pricked. Notice how different Snowline's neck and abdomen look between photos

Always reward your horse when he complies with your wishes, and he should soon understand what is required of him. Whenever he does not comply, simply repeat your instructions and withhold the reward. If you start to shout, or even to hit him you will get nowhere with him, and may as well give up. The ultimate aim is to have a horse that walks calmly into a correctly halted position upon command. This is achievable in most cases, and while the occasional horse may never understand what is required of him, this usually only happens when insufficient time has been spent in teaching what is required.

'As long as you practise enough at home, horses do soon get the idea of how to stand up properly and will almost walk straight into the correct stance in the ring,' says Allister. In fact they learn by repetition, and where a horse is unfortunately slow to learn, this may seem worse than watching paint dry! However, when in the ring, once your horse walks out of line and stands perfectly first time, you will be thankful for every day spent teaching him – and that is what showmanship is all about. Shows are won 75 per cent at home and only 25 per cent in the ring, and this is a conservative estimate!

Gauging whether a horse is standing correctly while you are mounted is more difficult, but you do need to be able to feel when he is standing correctly under you, without having to lean over and look down. At first it is helpful to have someone watch you from the ground, informing you when your

horse is standing correctly; then you can experience exactly how this feels, and can judge for yourself in the future when you achieve it.

Teaching the horse to stand correctly while mounted is also a little more difficult. It is accomplished by nudging a leg back or forth, rather than by asking him to move a pace forwards or backwards. To do this, apply pressure with your leg on the side you wish the horse's leg to move, and either give or resist the reins for a second or two. As soon as he begins to move his leg, you retake a normal contact and relax your leg; this should result in just the desired leg moving, and not the whole horse. If he does not appear to understand what you are asking, use a long schooling whip to tap the appropriate leg while giving the subtle aids for a backward or forward direction as discussed.

Having followed such procedures and taught the horse how to stand correctly both in-hand and ridden, the idea is to have him standing correctly every time you halt. This does not always happen, although once taught, most horses will adopt the correct position when requested to do so.

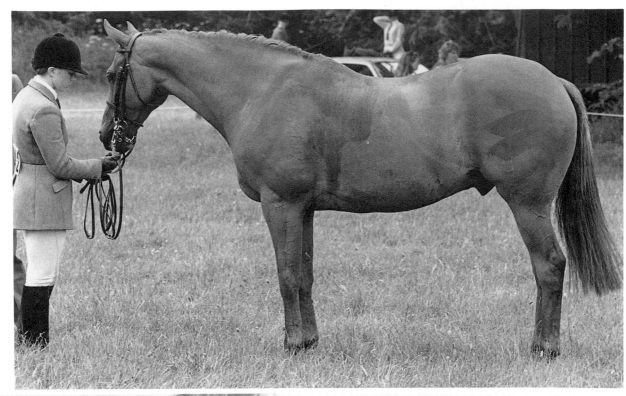

(Right and below) When standing a horse up while ridden you should be able to feel when his position is correct. Compare the top picture, which is totally wrong, to the bottom one. See how the horse's appearance has improved, just by having him stand correctly

(Left) Aquarius Spring Spice, a 15hh show hunter pony produced by Wendy and shown with great success by Kirsten Theobold. This horse was champion at Ponies UK in Peterborough. While he looks to be a nice type, he would improve his appearance if he were not standing so square. At present he has lost that 'look at me' quality

(Below left) Some US breeds, such as this American Saddlebred horse, have a totally unique stance (American Saddlebred Horse Association)

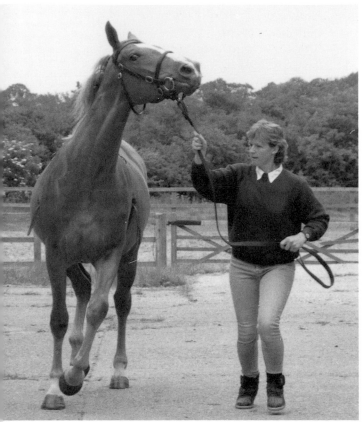

It is important to teach the horse to trot up correctly in-hand. When Wendy first started to train Snowline she would not trot straight, but would continually throw her head about. After a few sessions in side-reins Snowline soon realized what was required of her, and has never since reverted to her old behaviour

Teaching the Horse to Walk and Trot up Correctly

Providing a young horse has been taught to lead correctly, walking and trotting in-hand should cause few problems. Most problems occur with youngsters which are a little fresh, or become excited at the prospect of being out of their stable at home. In order to teach a horse to move in-hand you should have him in a proper in-hand bridle with a lead-line, or in a snaffle bridle with the reins taken over his head. If you know your horse is excitable, then it is a good idea to use a lunge-line as this will make it easier for you to keep hold of him should he play up. Stand at his near-side shoulder and have a schooling whip in your left hand. Ask him to walk on, and if he does not comply immediately, ask again and give a little flick of the whip around his rib area. Continue in this way until he moves on every time you ask. Do not turn around and pull at him, as this will only encourage him to pull backwards against you. In some cases it helps to have someone behind to encourage him forwards, but this practice should be dispensed with as soon as possible.

Once your horse is moving forwards in walk and trot on command, you can begin to concentrate on him being straight. Both Wendy and Allister use a hedge or fence line to achieve this, putting the horse between themselves and the fence, and then giving the command to walk or trot on, as desired. If a horse persists in not trotting straight, by turning his head in or pushing his quarters out, Wendy uses side-reins to combat the problem. 'As a yearling Snowline continually threw her head about,' explained Wendy, 'so I gave her a few sessions in side-reins. This stopped the problem, and now she trots up beautifully.' Such measures do have a lasting effect, especially if you teach the horse at a young age: no learning experience is ever wasted, and any time you spend teaching your horse such simple things is always valuable.

BASIC RIDDEN EDUCATION
Suppleness, Straightness and Transitions
You do not need access to top class facilities to show a horse; in fact much of your schooling work can be done while out riding. Both Wendy and Allister hack their horses out regularly, and accomplish on a hack much of the schooling work

that a dressage horse might do in the school. For instance, when simply walking along the road their horses are active and working from the leg to the hand, not just plodding along aimlessly.

Allister is keen to point out that his horses are continually being educated, whenever and wherever they are ridden. 'You just can't help it,' he says. 'It doesn't matter what you are riding, or whether it is at walk, trot or canter, you are always asking the horse to work properly. It is something that comes through force of habit, and you may not even realize you are doing it.'

A lack of purpose, however, is a very different thing, and it is a very common reason for schooling to seem both ineffective and boring; therefore it is important to set yourself some goals. Decide what you want to accomplish for each ride, and plan certain exercises to carry out en route. 'In this way the horse is learning and preparing for the show ring without associating it with being schooled – he is not being drilled round and round in circles,' Allister points out.

Such exercises may include:

• **Half-halts:** These can be used to help the horse balance himself, and to prepare for transitions if he is a little eager.
• **Transitions:** Choose a marker along the route where you plan to make a transition, and at the appointed place ride for an accurate and smooth one.
• **Halts:** Halting out on a hack is good for discipline. You should be able to ask for a halt any time, at any place, and your horse should comply. You will never know where you may have to halt in the ring, so it is as well for your horse to learn this lesson early.
• **Shoulder-in:** To help with suppleness, you can ride shoulder-in down a hedge line or even along a straight stretch of road. Once a young horse is

sufficiently developed to perform the movement, it is also an excellent way of dealing with shying. At a show there are often many objects lying around the ringside and you will not gain any marks if your horse keeps spooking at them.
• **Leg-yielding:** Similarly, leg-yielding is excellent for co-ordination and suppleness. Once the horse learns to leg-yield out on a ride, you can use the exercise to great benefit in the ring when approaching anything which might startle it.
• **Loops and serpentines:** If you have access to wide verges or grassy tracks you can perform loops and serpentines at both walk and trot. This will improve the horse's suppleness and straightness, and will help to establish correct bend.
• **Turns on the forehand and reining back:** These are a natural part of opening gates while out on a ride, and are movements which will help to keep the horse where you want him in the ring. Reining back may also be included in your individual show, so it is a valuable movement to learn in this natural way. An inexperienced rider may be in danger of encouraging the horse to rear if he tries to teach it in the school without the horse being properly prepared first.

CONSTRUCTIVE SCHOOLING

While most of the show horse's education can be accomplished away from any formal schooling area, inevitably some work will need to be done in the school in order to identify possible problems within an enclosed space, and to work on specific areas which need improvement. First, it is important to define your horse's particular schooling requirements: for example a hunter may need a different approach as compared to a hack. Next, a structured schooling programme must be planned in order to achieve these needs. It takes a little experience to judge when a horse would benefit from being taken in the school. Allister feels that after most horses have completed two or three weeks out hacking they could begin work in the school, although he stresses that each horse must be assessed individually. For example, some horses benefit from being schooled every day, just asking the same question until you get the right answer, then moving on by asking that little bit more; he considers that this seems to apply to new horses especially. 'All I am aiming for at this point is that the horse walks, trots and canters in a straight line and bends properly, carrying his head in the right position,' says Allister. 'The head carriage probably needs to be a little lower than is desirable for the show ring because when he gets in the ring the head will always come up anyway. It is important not to overdo it, though; if you do, you are in danger of having your horse very tight and tense in the ring. At the end of the day he has got to enjoy life!'

Most show horses need to improve in the following areas:

Calmness: In order to help your horse relax, first work on quite a long rein in walk. This will show him there is nothing to run away from, and if he is ridden by a judge who does not take a short contact

(Top left) Wendy gives Charlie a refresher lesson in trotting straight. Here she is not using the fence line as a barrier, as he knows how to trot up correctly

(Left) Most of the work that is usually done in a school can be accomplished while out hacking. Whatever horse she is riding, Wendy always makes sure that it is working, rather than just plodding along

Inevitably most horses do need some time in the school in order to highlight any problems which may become more apparent in an enclosed space. This also provides the opportunity for more detailed work on specific areas that need improvement

he will still be well behaved. Once he is relaxed in walk, you could progress to trot and canter on a long rein.

Suppleness: The show horse needs to be supple enough to stretch lengthways, in order to extend through the paces when asked. At first this is achieved by performing progressive upward and downward transitions on straight lines and circles, from walk to trot to canter, and from canter to trot to walk, for example. Once the horse is sufficiently supple, these transitions need no longer be progressive and the horse can be asked to go straight to walk from canter, or from halt to trot, for instance. Not only does this improve his suppleness further, it also sharpens the horse's reactions, making him more responsive to the aids.

Lateral suppleness is also important, especially for show hacks and riding horses. This is achieved by performing circles of decreasing size, loops, serpentines and changes of rein. The degree of lateral suppleness does not need to be perfected as for dressage, but the horse still needs to be able to keep the correct bend and not fall in or out when asked to turn.

Balance: Every show horse, no matter what class or category he fills, needs to be balanced: it is the balanced horse which gives the best ride, so work towards this end is always valuable. It helps to work on transitions between the paces, both progressive and non-progressive, and this can be taken one step further to include transitions within the gaits. Practise lengthening and shortening the strides within gaits (extending and collecting) – though be sure that the horse is not simply slowing down or hurrying; he still needs to have his hocks under him and be working through from behind. Work over poles and grids can help here, as can riding over undulating terrain. Hunting, or doing a few hunter trials, is a good way of educating the horse in this respect.

Straightness: Performing lateral movements will improve straightness, as will working away from the outside of the school track. Shoulder-in is a valuable exercise here, especially if performed on a circle, followed instantly by a few paces of lengthened stride.

Such early education will prepare your horse for the show ring in a progressive and focused manner. Any programme you plan must allow for alteration to suit the needs of the individual horse, but you should find that your sessions become more productive, purposeful and even enjoyable. Remember, the time you spend actually in the ring takes up very little of the week's exercise, so all the other work carried out at home and elsewhere must be enjoyable for both horse and rider.

The Paces

Once your horse is working calmly and willingly, you can begin to consider the quality of his paces. It is no good having the most beautiful-looking horse if it does not move well. The overall impression of movement is important, as it is this which catches the judge's eye and makes him say: 'Yes! This horse can really move!' It is difficult to define good movement, except to say that the horse should look to be light on his feet, perhaps even floating or dancing across the ground. The best way to observe this is to watch a horse with his blood up, parading in the field – then you will really see a horse that can move.

A horse that does not have good conformation (see Chapter 1) will never move as well as one that does. However, just because a horse is capable of good paces it does not mean that he will display them unless asked – and sometimes this has to be

with a firm boot! 'Before you can progress any further you must have your horse straight and forward-going,' says Allister.

At this point, it may be more beneficial to consider what it is the judge wants to see, rather than to discuss the merits or failings of individual horses; then you should be able to assess your own horse's strengths or weaknesses and to work upon them accordingly. If you find his paces are less than acceptable, then the exercises just discussed will help; but always make sure your horse is relaxed and in a good forward rhythm before increasing the amount of impulsion. Obviously there will be variation between the showing categories and between types of horse – US breeds will differ from UK and Australian breeds – but in general, good movement can be broken down into various factors.

The walk: The judge will want to see relaxed, swinging strides with the hind feet over-tracking. As the rhythm is four-time, he will want to observe four definite and even beats. While the head will move in time to the rhythm this should not be exaggerated and the horse should be still in his mouth.

The trot: Each of the steps should be light and elastic, with a long but rounded stride. A heavyweight hunter will not be as light as a hack, but he should still appear to spring from one pair of diagonals to the other, rather than dragging his feet along or having a high knee action. While lengthy strides are desirable, he will not want to see extended paces, unless this is during the individual show which is a requirement of some classes.

The canter: All too often you see horses cantering too fast in the show ring. The judge wants to see the horse bounding along, upwards and forwards with each stride, showing the ease with which he can keep the rhythm. The important thing is to strike off on the correct lead, so this must be practised at home. Generally if the horse is supple and well balanced, he will not find this difficult when coming off the corner.

The gallop: This pace is a faster version of the canter, but with lengthier strides, although the diagonal hind leg and foreleg move independently, making it a four-time pace. A good gallop is achieved through long, rhythmic strides rather than short, hasty ones; some horses are naturally good at

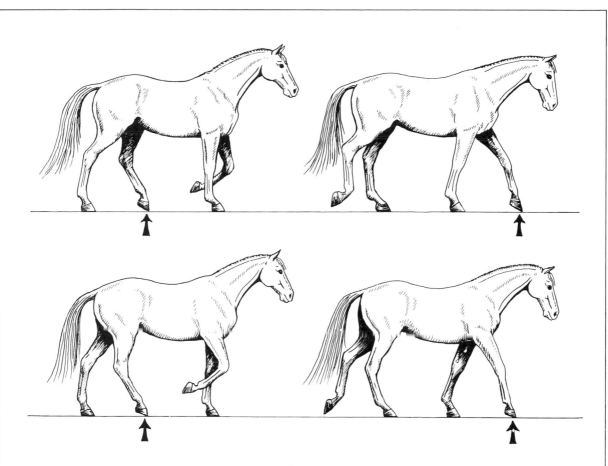

A good walk with four distinct beats is most important

A good gallop is achieved through long, rhythmic strides, rather than short, hasty ones

Once a good canter rhythm has been established, Wendy allows Charlie to lengthen into a gallop. Note the strain which is taken by any one leg; this is why it is so important that the horse is prepared well, before this fast pace is attempted

galloping, while others appear to tie their legs in knots. It is possible to educate the horse to gallop correctly, simply by teaching it to go away from the leg as soon as the aid is given; to lengthen, and then to come back as soon as the rider asks. This can be done while out hacking, or while in the field, providing the horse is under control. For the first gallop choose a smooth terrain which is free from pot-holes, or ditches in close proximity. It is also sensible to refrain from galloping in the same place each time, as this will encourage your horse to anticipate the gallop, which may lead to bolting if he becomes too excited. Galloping slightly uphill will encourage the horse to stop easily, as he will find it quite tiring.

In the ring you may only be able to show a few strides of gallop down the long side: the aim then is to make these strides of quality, rather than quantity. A horse which gallops with a quick, choppy stride is less desirable than one which may gallop more slowly, yet appears to glide along the ground. Speed excites a horse and this often leads to misbehaviour if it is not expertly contained, so you should aim to move forwards smoothly, allowing your horse to lengthen his stride rather than rushing him into a full-scale sprint.

Rapport between Horse and Rider

While a basic ridden education is essential for horses in all spheres of equestrianism, showing differs in that the horse must be easy for anyone to ride. He has got to be light in the hand, and must go forwards from the aids rather than as a result of anticipating what you want. It is a well known fact that some horses and riders can build up such a rapport that the rider hardly needs to give any aids before the horse has interpreted his or her wishes and come up with the right response. This 'hyper-sensitivity' or 'sixth-sense' can work against you in the show ring, so it is important to teach the horse to go from the leg and to act upon aids actually given, rather than on any of his rider's wishes that he might be able to sense.

In the early stages it is sensible for just one person to school the horse, then as the time for his first show approaches it is a good idea to have a few different people ride him so that he accepts other riders. It has been known for a horse to go perfectly for its usual rider, but to refuse to budge in the ring for the judge. This can be extremely embarrassing all round, and will certainly not result in many rosettes. While you may feel a judge should be experienced enough to ride any horse, on the day it is the horse which gives a smooth and willing ride that finds favour up the line. It makes sense, then, to provide your horse with the experience of other riders, that he may gain the knowledge to co-operate with any rider, at any time. This is a point often overlooked, and it can result in two or three wasted shows before the horse settles to the idea of someone else on his back.

While Wendy does all her horses herself, Allister has an added problem in that he produces horses for other riders; he therefore needs to judge how they will go for his clients, and to produce them with his clients' abilities, likes and dislikes in mind. 'Obviously you do not always gel with every horse you produce,' he says, 'but as long as you are aware of the situation you can counteract it by trying extra hard, relaxing yourself, or not trying at all, as the case may be. The onus is always on the rider to get on with the horse, not the other way around. At the end of the day the rider must learn to like the horse, and must learn to adjust to the horse's capabilities and individual characteristics.'

The US has many varied showing classes which require specific training. Here we see Jack the Zipper, a 15.1hh three-year-old stallion owned and ridden by Ann Carter of Heathlands Farms Quarter Horses, demonstrating the 'back-up' through L-shaped parallel poles, in full show gear

Gauging when the Horse is 'Right'

It is important to wait until your horse is physically and (perhaps more importantly) mentally developed until you show it for the first time. However, there comes a point when you need to take your horse to a show to complete his education. At first this will entail just taking him for a look around the showground, accustoming him to the sights and the sounds that make up the showing atmosphere. Once your horse has settled when he is taken out, you might try him in the ring, perhaps in a novice class if his experience or age warrants. At this point is it very important to try and pick a class with a judge that you know to be sympathetic and a quiet rider; those who have no experience of particular judges (see Chapter 10) should ask a friend to recommend a suitable class, and if you have no contacts then you will have to take pot luck, learning from each experience as you go. This might seem a little strange to those of you who have never shown before; after all, surely judges are judges because they are good at appraising horses and can ride them well, so why the need to pick and choose? The answer lies not in the riding ability of the judge, but in his or her sensitivity to particular types of horse. Some judges prefer a horse to take a strong hold and to be onward bound, while others appreciate a lighter, more delicate ride. Obviously if you have a horse which takes a strong hold it is more desirable to come up against the former judge; not only may you be placed higher in the line-up, but your horse will benefit from having an amiable ride. Professional show people will plan out their whole showing season months beforehand, matching closely the needs of their horses with the preferences of selected show judges.

Employing the Help of a Professional

There are many reasons for seeking the help of a professional, not least when things go wrong. However, we all slip into bad habits, so a keen eye on the ground every now and again can work wonders. The showing world is far less receptive to the idea of having regular coaching than other spheres of equestrianism, and certainly there are far fewer 'specialist' coaches here in the UK and Australia than in the United States.

'As long as you are confident with your riding, I wouldn't say it is always necessary to have lessons,' says Allister. 'However, you cannot actually see what the picture looks like – the one the judge will see – if you are doing it on your own, so it does help to have someone on the ground to offer advice. Anne will often watch me and advise that the horse needs to carry his head a little higher, or lower, or that it is trotting too fast or slow. It might feel all right to me, but if the visual picture is wrong, then it's wrong.' This also includes the rider. Where you may get away with your own style in showjumping or cross-country riding, in showing you have got to look stylish; the picture should always be one of effortless elegance.

Wendy will often call upon the help of Ruth McMullen to help her through a problem. 'A session with Ruth will help me to see where I am going wrong,' says Wendy, 'and then I can progress in the most effective way. It is pointless to struggle on alone, as the problem will escalate, and will then take twice as long to solve at the end of the day.'

No rider is ever so good that they have nothing to learn, and as Ruth says 'we are always learning throughout our lives, no matter how experienced we are with horses.' And that comes from a lady who has probably produced more champion horses and riders than anyone else in the UK.

4

PREPARATION

TRIMMING: READY FOR THE RING

For hunters, riding horses, hacks and show ponies, Anne and Allister trim out the ears, whiskers, jaws, heels and the top notch (about an inch section just behind the ears, where the headpiece of the bridle sits); these categories have their manes plaited and tails pulled for the ring. Cobs are also trimmed in the same way, and in addition have hogged manes. A good tip is not to hog the mane too near the day of the show if your horse's neck is slightly weaker than is desirable, as the extra growth of hair will help to bulk it up. However, a good strong neck will be enhanced by the streamlined appearance of a freshly hogged mane. In any event, do not leave a hogged mane longer than about two weeks without assessing the need to re-trim. Only use scissors at the bottom of the neck, because if the hair is trimmed too close to the skin at this point, the pressure of the horse's rugs may make him sore.

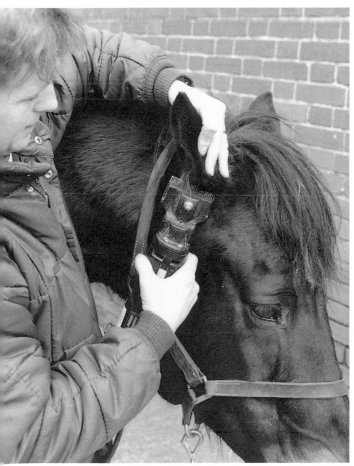

Apart from native ponies, most show horses have their ear hair...

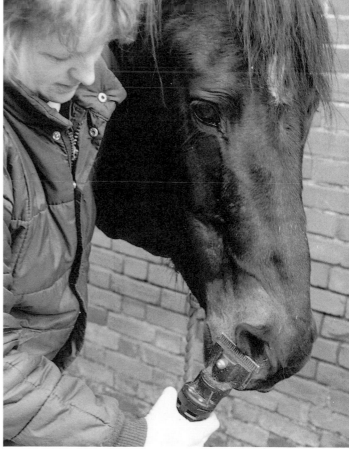

...and whiskers completely trimmed off. This can be done with the clippers if your horse will let you, or a pair of blunt-ended scissors

Flashes or shark's teeth put on just before entering the ring can enhance the quarters of a hunter and a cob; and quarter marks and possibly shark's teeth as well may be appropriate for a hack. The key is to enhance the horse in order to draw the judge's eye, but not to be too flashy so that he is bombarded by gimmicks which then only mask the horse. Mountain and moorland ponies and many 'breed' classes are shown in their natural state – that is, not trimmed, with flowing manes and tails (see Chapter 9). However, very thick, long and unruly manes can be thinned discreetly so that they lie correctly.

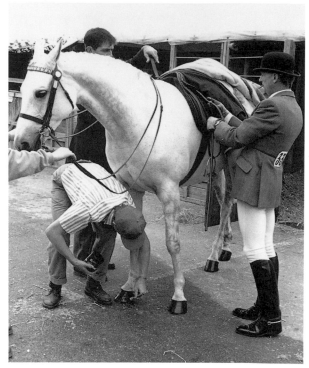

If your horse has good feet you can highlight them by blackening them, otherwise you might like to use just an ordinary hoof oil which produces a shine, but does not draw the eye

Many show people prefer not to bath their horses, but sometimes it is unavoidable

Many show people prefer not to bath their horses, and certainly not too regularly as this removes the natural coat oils, and thus the shine. For this reason it is never a good idea to bath a horse the day before a show. Washing the tail may be essential, but try not to wash the mane for a horse that is to be plaited, as this makes the job of plaiting far harder. As long as the horse is regularly groomed and well fed, a good brush over and strapping before the show should really make his coat shine.

Presenting a horse for the show ring is an art, and the task should not be under-estimated. As well as trimming and plaiting, you need to accentuate your horse's good features, and to try and minimize any coarse ones. For example, feet should be blackened if they are very good, but just lightly oiled if they are not the horse's strong point. The coat may be sprayed with sheen to make it sparkle, and a little baby oil or petroleum jelly may be put around the eyes and muzzle. However, a word of warning here – always make sure you also use a good fly repellent, as otherwise your horse may be plagued in the ring; and if the sun is shining beware of sunburn (you may need to use a sun block on pink areas). Where a horse's tail is a little thin and 'fly-away' a normal hair conditioner can help. Chalk or leg whitener can also be used to brighten a horse's white markings should he have any. Although they are obviously not 'natural', these finishing touches should be invisible to the overall appearance.

Whatever type of horse you are showing the objective is basically the same – you are trying to achieve a nice, sharp outline. This starts with trimming, but you need to stand back and take a good look at your horse first, to decide how to present him to his best advantage. For example, you do not want to use the clippers against the line of the hair on the back of the lower legs if your

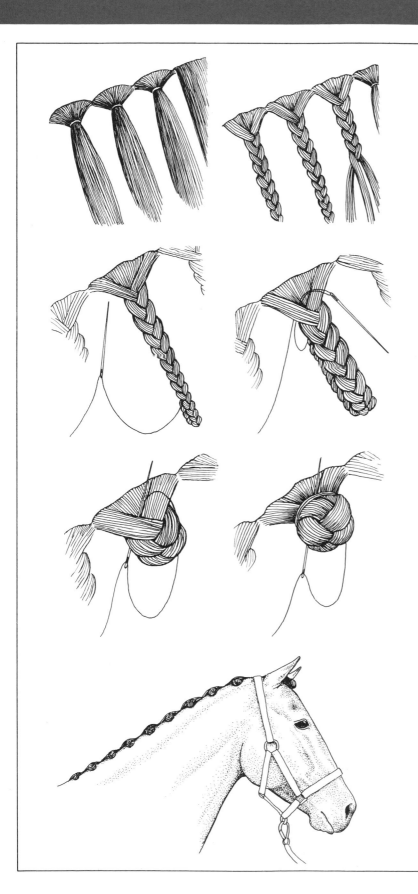

The correct way to plait with cotton and thread

• USING PLAITS TO ENHANCE APPEARANCE •
The number of plaits you use relates to the size of the horse's neck; generally hunter plaits may be a little larger with fewer along the neck, although this is not a rule and it is best to use whatever suits your horse. For example you can make a short neck look longer by using more, smaller plaits along the neck; and conversely fewer, large plaits can make a longer neck look shorter. Where you position the plaits will also create a certain effect: thus a weak top-line can be improved by sitting the plaits up along the crest of the neck, whereas a thick-set neck will be improved if the plaits are tucked neatly down to the side.

The number of plaits you use depends on the size of your horse's neck

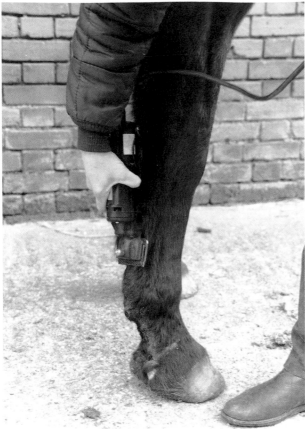

Take care when trimming that you are presenting your horse to his best advantage. On some horses' legs, it is sensible to use clippers...

...on others using a mane comb and scissors may be more appropriate

horse is fine boned, but you will want to for a cob with plenty of feather. Also, remember all the finishing touches, such as trimming round the coronets, and removing the whiskers and ergots.

When pulling, if you have a horse with a fine mane you will benefit from leaving it a little longer than for a thick mane; you can then still make reasonable-sized plaits, spacing them neatly along the neck . Nothing looks worse than hair stretched into a plait covering a few inches, because this is the only way to make a decent sized one; it does nothing to accentuate the horse's neck-line, and reflects badly on your presentation.

Tails should be banged, that is cut straight at the bottom. The correct length is for the tail to end between two and four inches (5 to 10cm) below the hocks, and bear in mind that many horses carry their tails high, so allow extra length when cutting the tail of such a horse. In ridden classes where exhibits are shown trimmed, it is usual to see a tail

pulled rather than plaited. Allister is a great believer in not brushing tails too regularly as this pulls too many hairs out and can ruin an otherwise lovely thick tail. To help with this problem you can use coat gloss on the tail after brushing to prevent it from tangling. All you then need to do is to run your fingers through the tail and any tangles will separate.

Where manes are plaited, these should be secured with cotton of a colour as similar to the mane as possible; white cotton on black or chestnut manes is fine for dressage, but it is definitely out for showing, as are rubber bands unless it is an emergency. Where a horse has been poorly clipped, or has had his mane badly pulled in the past, you may find he has short hairs that stick straight upwards along his crest. These can detract from the streamlined look you are trying to create, *but* you must never cut them off, or the problem will be twice as bad next time you come to plait. While

A thick mane can be pulled shorter than a finer mane in order to make plaiting easier

When pulling a mane, only pull it as short as you need to in order to plait it up neatly

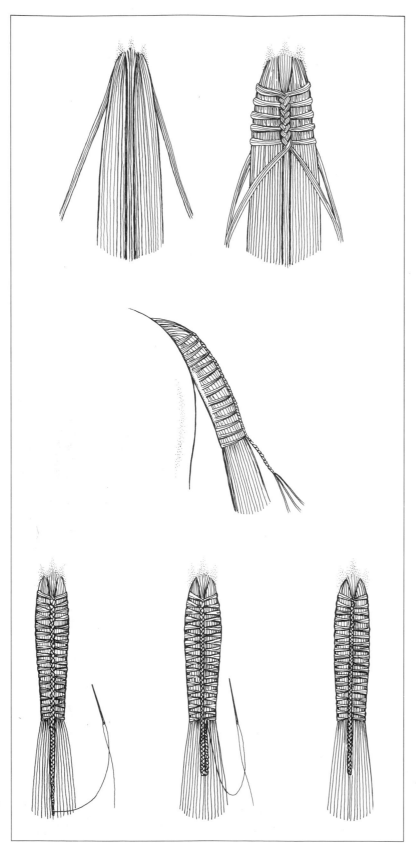

(Left) How to plait a tail

(Right) A very neatly pulled tail, which is always correct for hunters and most mainstream showing classes
(Far right) A plaited tail, which is more usual on youngstock
(Below right) Allister always likes to pull his horses' tails himself

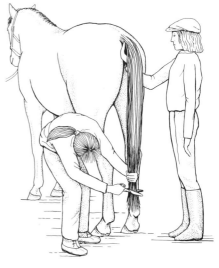

Trimming: holding the tail up will ensure the correct length when the horse holds his tail naturally when ridden

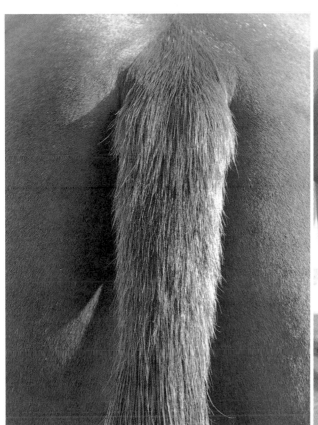

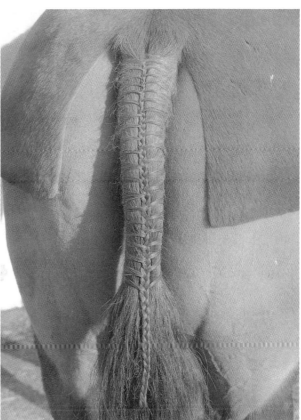

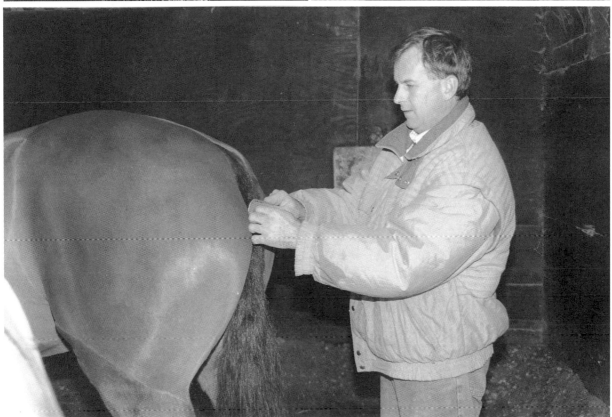

these hairs are growing out you can employ hair gel (for human use) to stick them down, without detriment to your horse's mane or his appearance as it doesn't show.

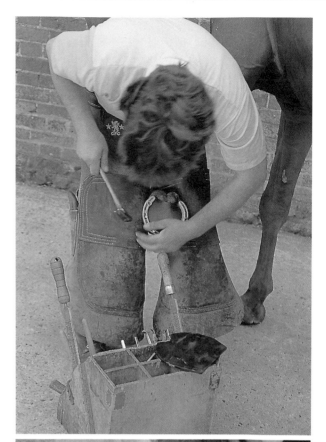

• **ROBERT OLIVER ON TRIMMING** •
Take care with trimming, as it makes so much difference to the horse's appearance. I trim off everything for a stabled horse. A horse at grass can still be trimmed when shown, but not to the same degree of finesse as a stabled horse. Regular attention to your horse's feet is also very important as the feet must always be right, for showing and all other activities.

An Overview of Australian Presentation

Caroline Wagner, one of the stars of the Australian scene for many years (see page 74), gives her comments on presentation: 'Along with softer plaits in the mane, the look for tails has also changed, to be shorter and not over-full. The length is now up to just below the hocks, whereas a few years ago it was down closer to the fetlocks. Another general presentation change is the use of ribbon browbands with ribbon rosettes and flags at either side; these are used a lot on hacks and galloways (see page 74), as well as riding ponies.'

HEALTH AND CONDITION

A horse only needs to be fit enough to do the job of showing; if he is too fit he may be too full of himself in the ring. However, the important thing is to consider whether the horse is too fat or not: if he is fit and well conditioned, he can carry a fair bit of weight as long as much of that condition is muscle rather than fat. But if you are not careful to keep

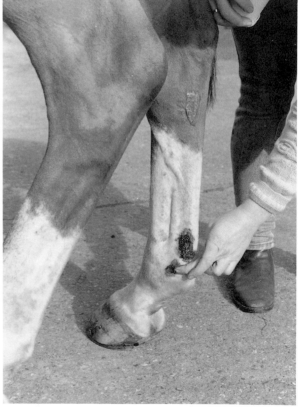

(Top) Regular attention to the horse's feet is very important as the feet must always be right for showing. This horse is being fitted with a leather pad to protect the sole which in this horse bruises easily

(Right) Regular attention to detail is important if the horse is to look his best when he reaches the ring. Small ailments such as mud fever should be 'nipped in the bud' before they get out of hand

your horse ticking over in between shows, he will probably get 'flabby fat' and this is the sort of condition that just falls off when you start travelling. 'Achieving and maintaining good muscle condition by correct feeding and appropriate work is most important if you are to have the show horse in the right condition for the job,' says Allister.

According to Australia's Caroline Wagner, the conditioning of Australian show horses has changed over the years. At one time show horses tended to be just fat, rather than well muscled, and they were often overweight. These days people keep their horses much fitter and in much better muscle tone, and this allows horses to move better and more freely. 'After all, a good show hack should cover the ground easily and smoothly,' she says.

PRELIMINARY PREPARATIONS

Organizing yourself

Being prepared for the show season means not only ensuring that you and your horse are ready, but also that all the paperwork and administrative details are carried out in plenty of time so there are no last-minute panics.

You need to ensure that your horse's equine influenza and tetanus injections are up to date, and that its vaccination record has been completed correctly by your veterinary surgeon; without it you may not be able to enter the showground. If your horse is a small hunter, or in a class that is restricted by height, you should organize an assessment of your horse by a vet to obtain a height certificate – this will certainly be needed at affiliated shows, and may prevent any doubts at smaller shows as to your horse's eligibility for a class. Should you wish to enter any major shows, you should send off for their schedules early in the year, as generally these entries close many weeks ahead of the show. February is not too soon to start thinking about this, so be prepared with envelopes and stamps. Make sure that the owner, the rider and the horse are all registered with the appropriate society if necessary, and study all the rules and regulations carefully so that you do not get caught out on the day. Once you have registered, the society will automatically send you a list of its

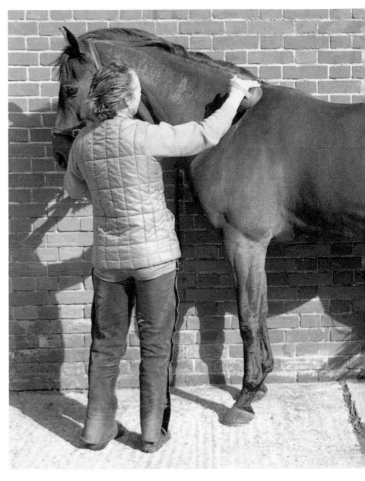

Achieving and maintaining good muscle condition by correct feeding, strapping and appropriate work is most important in order to have the show horse in the right condition for the job

rules and regulations (see Appendix for addresses.) Check that your horsebox or trailer and towing vehicle are in good repair, roadworthy and legal. If you do not have your own transport, now is the time to try and arrange shared transport or the hire of a suitable vehicle.

Showground Education

Showground education is when you accustom your horse to all the new sights and sounds he will encounter while at a show, without actually expecting him to perform. This process is commonly called 'taking him for a jolly', and helps to ease him into the world of showing without making him too anxious or excited. For his first outing you might just take him to a small local

How quickly a horse settles to the showing environment depends on his personality and how well he has been prepared. This is Mystic Minstrel behaving impeccably when faced with the crowd at Wembley

show to let him have a look round; it need not be a showing show, just one where there are other horses, spectators, loud hailers and so on. Having settled the horse to this environment, you can then progress on his next trip and perhaps take him into a best turned out class, or a clear round jumping.

• DRESS REHEARSALS •

Moggy and Sally Hennessy always take their youngsters out for a look before they actually compete. 'Sometimes we take them down to Poplar Park in Suffolk where there is a BHS event course to jump some of the cross-country fences, or else we take them to a small local show where they can let off steam without it mattering too much!'

How quickly a horse settles to the environment depends upon his individual personality, but it is never fair to expect a young or novice horse to go out and perform well in a class the very first time he attends a show.

Tips from Australia

Australia's Maureen Walker (see page 128) provides some top tips for young competitors, and for those people who want to start showing their horse but don't know how to get involved:

1 Find a friend or teacher to help.
2 Go to shows with these people to help them, and to watch how it is all done in order to learn about the preparation required and the procedure.
3 Knowing what is expected will also help you to assess whether you are ready or not.
4 Prepare yourself, your equipment and your horse as well as possible, choose one of the smaller shows, and then off you go! Nothing teaches like competition.
5 Remember, win or lose, *always smile!* Everyone

gets beaten, but that is what makes winning more rewarding.

6 Success comes down to the following criteria: how hard you work, how well you do it, how good your horse is, and your own determination to grow in your chosen field and continually get better.

7 A sense of humour and a positive attitude are your best aids.

THE IMPORTANCE OF MANNERS

• ROBERT OLIVER'S TOP TIP •

*Paying attention to detail is most important: see to every little detail, **all** the time. And manners are essential – ensure you teach them to your horse **before** you attempt to show him. A horse's manners 'in the country' seem to have been lost, yet such manners should be a fundamental part of training the show horse. Lots of riders can ride their horse in a school, but to do so nicely across country, without getting too deep into the dressage aspects and while still making him do as he is told, is very important. Teaching manners to in-hand stock is also essential if your horses are to trot up, stand still and generally behave themselves when in the ring.*

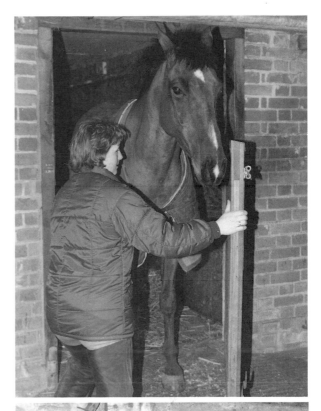

'Manners are often something that either a horse has naturally, or he does not,' says Allister. 'However, his manners at home may be quite different from his manners at a show. While a horse may be well mannered and respectful at home, there is no telling how the show environment will affect him, so you cannot start to get cross with an otherwise well mannered horse if he becomes excitable at a show. Such a horse will just need to be worked a lot more before his class so that he learns to settle. You just have to know your horse and be prepared accordingly.'

Manners at home are extremely important, as they will reflect how much respect a horse will have for his handler when out. This horse decided he wanted to barge straight past Wendy...but after a little lesson he decides he had better do as he is told. This was achieved by simply repeating the command to stand, and scolding the horse each time he tried to barge

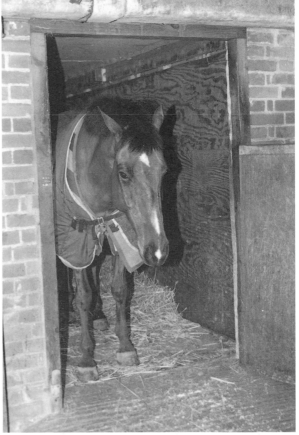

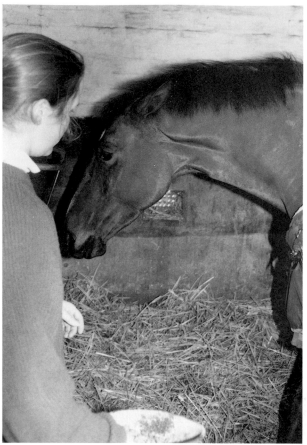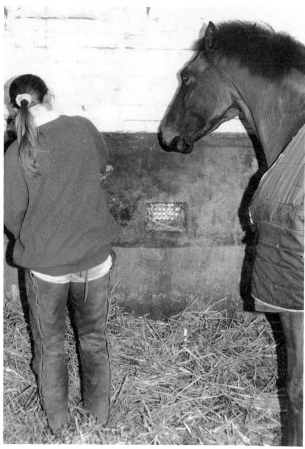

(Left) While some horses do get very uppity when it comes to feed times, it is not unreasonable to expect them to wait until you are ready
(Right) They must realize that you are the boss – although you must be a fair one, otherwise the horse will soon start to become despondent

When asked 'How highly do you rate manners in a show horse?' Vin Toulson replied:

'Manners are all-important in the show ring. A show horse should be well schooled, and it should also have a naturally good temperament; not only should it go well for its rider, it should also give the judge a good mannerly ride. In addition, if it is to go right to the top it should be a natural "show-off" who genuinely enjoys showing. The real champions will learn to extend their paces down the stand side of the ring without any prompting from their riders. Seabrook and Assurance are true examples of this, and Assurance would even squeal if he thought he was not getting adequate attention!

'Most regrettably some top horses have recently been settled down by the use of sedatives, and it is essential that the British Show Hack, Cob and Riding Horse Association and the National Light Horse Breeding Society clamp down hard, with random blood tests and severe penalties to eradicate this practice. The pony showing societies have already done so.'

5

HORSES FOR CLASSES

In the United Kingdom there are literally hundreds of showing classes, so anyone with any horse can have a go, from a Shetland to a Shire. Ridden showing is divided into two sections:
• **Types**, of which hunters, show ponies and cobs are examples; and
• **Breeds**, of which Arabians (always referred to as Arabs), Welsh ponies and Connemaras are examples.

The most prestigious showing classes in the UK for horses are the hunter weight divisions, followed closely by the hacks, cobs and riding horses. These classes are always well supported by exhibitors, and there are always many spectators around the ringside. For the pony, the most prestigious are the show pony classes (a 'type' rather than a 'breed'), and it is not unusual for there to be so many competitors that they are almost nose to tail in the ring! In certain areas, one particular breed dominates: Welsh ponies and cobs are very popular in Wales, for instance, but classes for the breeds are also held at most major agricultural shows.

The showing scene is vast, and one book alone cannot hope to cover each and every type and breed and do it justice. What follows is therefore an overview of mainstream ridden showing in the UK. (An overview of the breeds and in-hand showing is given in Chapter 9.)

CLASSES RUN UNDER NATIONAL LIGHT HORSE BREEDING SOCIETY RULES (HIS)

Hunters

In the UK the 'weight' hunters are fairly big horses. Basically, a **lightweight** should be able to carry 12st 7lb (80kg), although in reality many can take more weight than this. Although there are no stipulations regarding amount of bone or height, as a general guide a lightweight should be between 16hh and 16.1hh, with no less than 8in (20cm) of bone. A lightweight does have to have a fair bit of quality and give a very good ride because it should be able to double as a ladies' horse if required.

A **middleweight** hunter is a step up in size and should have more bone. It should have a good depth of girth in order to carry a bigger person, being capable of carrying over 12st 7lb (80kg), though not exceeding 14st (89kg). It need not be as elegant as a lightweight, but should still be handsome and well mannered. As a general guide a good sort will be around 16.1hh to 16.2hh with 8½in (21cm) or more of bone.

A **heavyweight** hunter is a much bigger horse altogether, one that should be able to carry a big, heavy man across any country; affiliated classes expect such a horse to be capable of carrying over 14st (89kg) without any problem. This does not mean he should be a carthorse though; as a general guide a good sort would be 16.2hh or over, with no less than 9in (23cm) of bone. All hunters should be good movers whatever their category, and they should all have presence and appeal. They are always judged as a group – that is, they are not required to give an individual show as are hacks or riding horses.

Where there are only two classes scheduled, the weights are split as: lightweight, capable of carrying 13st (82.5kg) and under, and heavyweight, capable of carrying over 13st (82.5kg). All horses in the weight classes should be mares or geldings of four years old or over.

Small hunters are those which are 15.2hh and under (half an inch /1.2cm is allowed for ordinary shoes). The horse must be measured, and must hold a 'Joint Measurement Scheme Height Certificate' in order to compete at affiliated shows. A horse cannot compete in both a small hunter class, and a weight class at the same show.

A **ladies' hunter** may be a mare or gelding suitable to carry and be ridden by a lady side-saddle. There are many that compete in the lightweight classes, but you do also see some of the middleweights doubling as ladies' hunters.

Novice hunter classes are restricted to horses that have not won a certain amount of prize money at affiliated shows.

Four-year-old hunter classes are, as their name suggests, restricted to horses of four years old in the current year.

Working hunters may be mares or geldings, four years old or over, that exceed 15hh in height. They are required to jump a course of fences that have a natural appearance and are not easily dislodged. The class is judged 50 per cent on jumping performance and 50 per cent as for the weight hunter classes. The horse's manner of going is taken into account, with refusals being severely punished. Where entries permit, classes are often split into two weight categories: horses capable of

(Above) A lightweight must have a fair bit of quality and give a good ride, and should therefore be able to double as a ladies' horse if required. Here we see Wendy riding Mr R.D. Colson's Colgrove, winning at the East of England Show (Anthony Reynolds)

(Right) Mr R.D. Colson's Claybank Don, produced and ridden by Wendy as a middleweight. He was a consistent winner in the ring, coming fifth at Wembley twice (Anthony Reynolds)

carrying 13st (82.5kg) and under, and over 13st. Any show hunter should also be able to do working hunters; all they need is the scope to jump the fences in good hunting style. They should not jump like a showjumper, but should just stride on and take each fence as it comes up.

Unaffiliated classes are generally run under similar rules, stipulating the same requirements for competitors, although horses need not be registered.

(Above) A heavyweight hunter is expected to carry over fourteen stone (89kg) without any problem. This is Vin Toulson riding Oliver IV at the 1994 Royal Norfolk Show; a fine example of a heavyweight hunter by Skippy

(Left) Maggie Davies' Bee Master is a lovely pattern of horse for a working hunter. In 1994 he qualified for both the Royal International and Wembley. He is also a good all-rounder, proving his worth in dressage, showjumping and eventing

(Above) Some classes provide a lot of fun for both competitors and spectators. This is the 'hunt teams relay' in which horses are judged in the way they perform as a team

• THE IDEAL SHOW HORSE •

'The ideal show horse probably does not exist,' says Sally Hennessy, 'although Moggy is lucky enough to have one that must be pretty near the mark in College Jester. Not only is he a lovely lightweight, but he is a top ladies' horse, and a useful working hunter, too. Moggy and I, however, would probably choose a horse from the 1970s as our pattern of a perfect show hunter: a lightweight called Heron's Phase, a horse ridden by Ruth McMullen for Paul Rackham; he was a bay Thoroughbred of great quality, wonderful manners and great movement. King's Warrior must also feature in this list as he is such a wonderful mover and a horse with an impeccable temperament.'

CLASSES RUN UNDER THE BRITISH SHOW HACK, COB AND RIDING HORSE ASSOCIATION

Riding horses

There are two categories of riding horse: **small** (exceeding 14.2hh but not exceeding 15.2hh) and **large** (over 15.2hh). The small riding horse is basically a cross between a hack and a small hunter. It needs to be a good mover, but need not be as steady as a small hunter or as dainty as a hack. Although technically the large riding horse can be any height over 15.2hh, it has basically filled the gap between 15.2hh and 16.1hh where the lightweight hunters start. The large riding horse needs to be a nice horse of around that height, and one which anyone should be able to ride out. When judging the riding horse the emphasis is on manners, ride and training. As with hunter classes, riding horses are required to gallop in the ring. Once in a preliminary line, the judge will ride the horses; he will then require each one to give an

Kingfisher, Champion Riding Horse with Allister. In his first season (1994) he either won or was placed at most county shows

individual show which should not exceed one and a half minutes. Sometimes, however, there may not be time for an individual show, or at least not for those horses further down the line. When requested, the show should include the walk, trot and canter, a simple change of canter and rein-back; the horse should be able to strike off on the required leg, gallop on, halt obediently and stand still.

Other riding horse categories include the **novice riding horse**, for horses which have not won a first prize of a specified amount; novice riding horses may be ridden in a snaffle. There is also the **ladies' side-saddle class** and the **under 25s** (where the rider's age is between 15 and 24 years inclusive on the 1 January of the current year). Both these last two categories also apply to hacks and cobs.

Hacks

As with riding horses, there are two hack categories: **small** (exceeding 14.2hh, but not exceeding 15hh) and **large** (exceeding 15hh, but not exceeding 15.3hh).

The small hack should be stockier than the large hack because it still has to carry an adult; it tends to have pony or Arab blood in order to keep the height down. The hack must be a pleasure to ride: it should have excellent manners, be in easy self-balance, and ride light to the hand. When judging conformation, the emphasis should be on quality and elegance. The elegance required stems from a well set on head and neck, combined with a good length of shoulder, and the movement should be smooth and graceful with a true pointing toe. To achieve these qualities the hack must be extremely

• RIDING HORSE OR HUNTER? •

'Riding horses can be such a mixed bag that it is difficult to have an "ideal" stamp of riding horse,' says Sue Rawding.' There have been one or two instances where a successful show hunter has had the weight stripped off it, and it has then been shown successfully as a riding horse – and vice versa, where a riding horse has been "upgraded" to become a hunter. In fact a horse cannot be both, but the problem is that the lightweight hunters have become far too big. For me, the ideal riding horse is one that is sensible and well mannered enough to carry all members of the family; the children, and Mum and Dad!'

well schooled so that each movement looks effortless. A system of judging is adopted which awards 40 per cent for conformation, presence, type and action in-hand, and 60 per cent for ride, training test and manners.

As with riding horses, there are also categories for **novice**, **ladies' side-saddle** and **under 25s**.

• THE TRUE HACK •

'Years ago a hack was an animal that a gentleman would ride to the hunt meet; he would then switch to his hunter for the chase, and change back at the end of the hunt to hack home,' says John Rawding. 'We have definitely lost this stamp of a hack; after all, this was able to carry a fairly big man. In fact, many of the riding horses we see in the ring today are the "covert" hacks of yesteryear. The small hacks today are far too spindly and flighty – they are just overgrown ponies. They should be a nice Thoroughbred type with plenty of limb that will carry twelve or thirteen stone – whereas half of today's small hacks wouldn't carry your boots!'

Cobs

Cobs are a type of horse, rather than any specific breed. They are short-legged animals that exceed 14.2hh, but do not exceed 15.1hh. While fairly short, they should still have the bone and substance of a heavyweight hunter, and although they should be capable of carrying a substantial weight they should still have plenty of quality. They should be well mannered, and suitable for nervous or elderly riders. A cob has a sensible head, sometimes Roman-nosed; a full, generous eye; a shapely neck – crested on the top, with hogged mane – and well defined withers; and clean, strong hocks. It should have all the attributes of a good hunter, including low movement and being comfortable to ride, and it should not pull. Cobs are judged in the same manner as hunters, and they should be well schooled, and particular attention should be paid to manners. There are two weight categories: lightweight (capable of carrying up to 14st (89kg) with 8½in (21cm) of bone) and heavyweight (capable of carrying over 14st, with at least 9in (23cm) of bone). Other categories include:

Working cob (including both weights)**:** There

Hamlet, a horse only acquired in May 1994 and who was only lightly shown, yet he managed to stand Novice Champion at the British Show Hack, Cob and Riding Horse Association's National Show at Arena UK. He went on to be Supreme Champion at the show, and came fourth at Wembley

This picture epitomizes the power, yet grace of a show cob: Tom Cobbley, a lightweight cob, owned and ridden by Cathryn Scott and produced by Allister. Here they are on their way to coming third at Wembley 1994

• WHERE ARE THE HEAVYWEIGHTS? •

John Rawding is not alone in feeling that for some reason all ridden show horses have gone up a league; and most of the UK's professionals agree! The average riding horse should really be a lightweight hunter; the lightweight hunter a middleweight; and the middleweight hunter a heavyweight. 'As it stands now, where do you get your heavyweights from?' says John. 'They need to be so big to compete that they just cannot be bred, and this is why it is not unusual to see only three heavyweights in a class at county shows.'

'There is a tendency for horses to be too tall as well,' says Sue Rawding. 'For example, it is not uncommon to see a 17.1hh horse in the lightweights, when really your ideal horse in this category should be about 16.1hh or 16.2hh maximum. As the good heavyweights have fallen by the wayside, so has the true stamp of small hunter – if you could breed some of these you would really be making some money! There hasn't really been anything to match Smallprint for a very long while,' says Sue. John agrees wholeheartedly: 'If you could breed good small hunters you would really be making a fortune, without any shadow of a doubt,' he says.

THE ARAB HORSE SOCIETY

Arab classes are run for pure Arabs, Anglo-Arabs (Thoroughbred x Arab) and part-bred Arabs (those that have a minimum of 25 per cent Arab blood). Classes for Anglo and part-bred Arabs may be mixed. Undoubtedly, Arabs are a breed that you either love or hate. Although there are no definite guidelines, most Arabs are between 14.2hh and 15hh, and they are always termed 'horses' even if they are under 14.2hh. An Arab's fine, delicate looks characterize it from other show horses, although this belies the fact that they can be exceptionally strong with plenty of stamina. A good sort of Arab has a delicate, sculptured head with a dished nose, and a high, flighty tail carriage. Anglo and part-bred Arabs often take on some of these characteristics, although to a lesser degree. They are shown with flowing manes and tails – that is, neither pulled, nor plaited. Many Anglo- and part-bred Arabs also show in hack and riding horse classes, where they are turned out as appropriate for these classes.

RIDDEN PONY CLASSES

Ridden mountain and moorland

There are nine 'native' breeds in the UK, all of which are excellent types in their own right, but which also serve as valuable foundation stock for cross-breeding with Thoroughbreds and other breeds. The generic term for all these breeds is 'mountain and moorland', and this is the name given to many classes that are open to all the breeds. However, mixed mountain and moorland classes may be divided into large breeds and small ponies (see Chapter 9).

> **• MOUNTAIN & MOORLAND CLASSES •**
> *Large mountain and moorland breeds encompass the Dales, Highland, Fell, Connemara, New Forest, Welsh ponies of cob type (Section C, Welsh Cobs), Section D and Welsh ponies (Section B).*
> *Small mountain and moorland ponies encompass the Exmoor, Dartmoor, Shetland and the Welsh Mountain (Section A).*

are two divisions for the working cob, novice and open – the jumps do not exceed 3ft (0.9m) in height and 3ft 6in (1.0m) in spread for the novice, and 3ft 3in (0.97m) in height and 3ft 9in (1.1m) in spread for the open.

Novice show cob: Not to have won a first prize over a certain amount in straight show cob classes.

Open cob: A class that includes both weight divisions competing against each other.

Amateur owner/rider class: For those riders deemed to have amateur status as stipulated by the BSHC & RH Association.

Ladies' side saddle.

Under 25s.

(Top) An Arab shown in his 'natural state'. Arab classes are for pure Arabs, Anglo-Arabs and part-bred Arabs

(Left) Cosford Chaucer, a Section A Welsh Mountain pony who achieved Champion Novice Mountain and Moorland at the Ponies UK show in 1994, ridden by Harry Hood and led by Allister

Each native breed has its own society (see Appendix), which is responsible for the registration of ponies, and promotion of the breed. It can be extremely difficult to judge a mountain and moorland class as there may be first class examples of each breed forward – so how do you select a winner? Again, it comes down to personal preference. Obviously it is preferable to have specific breed classes, and this does happen in areas where the breed prevails. Moreover all societies hold at least an annual breed show, if not more regular shows in various counties throughout the year.

Ridden show ponies

Ridden show ponies are a type, not a breed. They can be one of the native breeds, but more usually they are cross-bred, with some Thoroughbred blood. The British show pony often looks like a miniature Thoroughbred, and it is greatly admired around the world. However, it is rarely reproduced in other countries, except perhaps the USA where some have been imported, as it is felt these animals are too fine, and fragile for the child rider who should really be having fun learning to ride over all sorts of terrain. This is why there are two schools of thought on ridden show ponies. Those that participate would defend the fact that their children have fun and do it for the pleasure they receive; those that do not say

Fieldcote White Wig, a good all-round pony seen here coming second in a lead-rein class first time out with Alexander King (Event Print)

that small children are often made to sit on professionally produced ponies, just so that 'Mrs Jones' can keep up with 'Mrs Smith'. An unfair view perhaps, but it cannot be denied that more smiles emanate from the native and working hunter pony riders' faces than from those on the ridden show ponies.

Classes are for ridden show ponies, working hunter ponies, and show hunter ponies:

Ridden Show Pony Categories

Leading rein: Ponies to be four years and over, not exceeding 12hh. Riders not to have attained their seventh birthday before 1 January in the current year.
Open first ridden: Mare or gelding, four years old and over, not exceeding 12hh. Riders not to have attained their tenth birthday before 1 January in the current year.
Ridden show pony: Four years and over, not exceeding 12.2hh, riders not to have attained their thirteenth birthday before 1 January in the current year.
Ridden show pony: Four years and over, over 12.2hh but not exceeding 13.2hh, riders not to have attained their fifteenth birthday before 1 January in the current year.
Ridden show pony: Four years and over, over 13.2hh but not exceeding 14.2hh, riders not to have attained their seventeenth birthday before 1 January in the current year.

Working Hunter Pony Categories

Working hunter pony: Pony four years and over, exceeding 14hh but not exceeding 15hh. Riders not to have attained their 20th birthday before 1st January in the current year.
Working hunter pony: Pony four years and over, exceeding 13hh but not exceeding 14hh. Riders not to have attained their seventeenth birthday before 1 January in the current year.
Working hunter pony: Pony four years and over, not exceeding 13hh. Riders not to have attained their fourteenth birthday before 1 January in the current year.
Nursery working hunter pony: Pony four years and over, not exceeding 13hh. Riders not to have attained their twelfth birthday before 1 January in the current year.

Show Hunter Pony Categories

Pony of show hunter type: Mare or gelding, four years old and over, exceeding 12hh but not exceeding 13hh. Riders not to have attained their fourteenth birthday before 1 January in the current year.

Pony of show hunter type: Mare or gelding, four years old and over, exceeding 13hh but not exceeding 14hh. Riders not to have attained their seventeenth birthday before 1 January in the current year.

Pony of show hunter type: Mare or gelding, four years old and over, exceeding 14hh but not exceeding 15hh. Riders not to have attained their twentieth birthday before 1 January in the current year.

AUSTRALIAN CLASSES

Classes for show horses in Australia are very different from in the UK. In major horse shows, classes are held for small ponies (below 12.2hh), large ponies (below 14hh), galloways (14–15hh), and hacks (over 15hh). Each section usually has 2in (5cm) divisions, with the championship class consisting of the winners of each height division, for example the novice small pony 11.2hh and not exceeding 12hh, or the open hack 15hh and not exceeding 15.2hh. Hunter classes – lightweight, middleweight and so on – are generally unheard of at official level. Most ponies are termed riding, Australian or Welsh; many galloways are Australian stock horses, Quarter Horses, riding ponies or small Thoroughbreds, and the vast majority of hacks are Thoroughbreds, many of which have been bought off the racecourse; for many years this has been the most efficient and cheapest way of acquiring horses for the show ring in Australia. Caroline Wagner describes the Australian scene:

'Horses that are shown in Australia have changed in general. We don't see the heavier horses with more bone that used to be shown any more and this goes right through the heights, from ponies to galloways and finally hacks. Riding ponies have had a big influence in the pony and small galloway sections, with the heavier types just not being as popular. The fact that there are not the classes for

Champion Australian Arabian stallion 1994, Espiration (Michael Vink)

Caroline Wagner and the spectacular Ark Royal. This horse is one of Australia's great hacks (Kate Ames)

the heavyweight types at the Royal Show any more has also played its part in these changes. When the classes changed to open heights, only the heavier weight horses with more bone had trouble competing directly with the finer boned and generally prettier horse. We simply don't have the hunter or cob classes as in the UK. Our hacks compete from 15hh upwards in 2in divisions. The over 16.2hh hack is a big horse, but he is still basically the same type of fine Thoroughbred that the 15hh–15.2hh horse is. Our show horses over 14.2hh are generally Thoroughbreds that have been bred to race and have often been too slow or small to race well. We also get a proportion who race very well, but are geldings, so their next career may be as a show horse if looks, conformation and temperament permit.

'This is often the reason that our show horses are exhibited much later in life. They may show until they are fifteen or sixteen years old, and still at the top level if kept in super show condition. They may have raced until they are seven or eight, or simply have been tried at the racetrack until they are five-year-olds; these racing experiences unfortunately do nothing to help the transition to becoming a show hack! However, the racing world does provide us with some wonderfully bred, beautiful Thoroughbreds, as we really do not have a breeding programme for show horses over 14.2hh in Australia.'

The Arabian and Quarter Horse industries are both very strong in Australia and are influenced by the United States. Both associations have memberships of around 5,000 and the horses are shown in-hand and under saddle within the boundaries of their own breed. Very few Arabians are shown under saddle, for example in open hack classes. Quarter Horses are more versatile, and are often shown as galloways and hacks, some having done so with great success. Quarter Horses are at a slight disadvantage in open company due to the fashion which favours lighter-boned horses, although this is not a rule.

Riding pony breeders, and Australian and Welsh pony breeders are active and strong in their promotion, and many overlap into the ridden show horse industry. There are basically two markets for these horses and ponies: to Pony Club children, and to the show horse community, and these two markets are adequately and actively sought.

Allister's view of the Australian showing scene

Allister has had first-hand experience of the Australian showing scene:

'I was just rung up from Australia out of the blue and asked whether I would consider judging out

there. I went, and found it a fantastic experience, and I continue to go now. In Australia and the USA showing categories are different from each other, and from here in the UK. In Australia there are lots of classes for 'equitation' and 'turnout', which are judged far more on the rider and overall presentation, rather than on the horse, so literally any person could show in these classes, with whatever horse they happened to have.

'Large hacks in Australia range from anything up to what would be almost a lightweight hunter in the UK, from 15hh upwards. In many ways the Australian scene is in front of the UK, but in other ways it is behind us. They have got some really lovely horses. When I judged the hacks over there, the first three that I chose would have been absolutely top class hacks in the UK – you don't often get three top class hacks in one class here in the UK, unless of course you are at Wembley or the Royal International. The class for galloways is another category which can be difficult to judge. When I judged there, I had four horses that in the UK would be small hacks, and four horses that would be classed as show or working hunter ponies, all in this same class. I preferred the small hack types, and luckily for me they did all behave and perform nicely; the others did as well, but the hack-types did nothing to put themselves down.

'The large hacks were a varied bunch, ranging from what would be large hacks in the UK, but also riding horses and a couple of lightweight hunters, all in the same hack class. Judges have to assess horses very much on the way they go for their own riders, as judges do not ride the exhibits in Australia; the horses do their "workout" – what would be an individual show in the UK – and you judge it on that. I did ride them, however, and it was significant that at the finish I ended up with two very equal horses and it was, in fact, the ride that tipped the balance on the day for the winner.

'The Australian workouts require a very high standard of horsemanship. When I was judging, nearly all the horses performed flying changes, and displayed paces that would only be seen in the dressage arena in the UK, so that aspect of showing is higher than in the UK. However, their riders' own dress sense and turnout was way behind the UK riders, whereas the horses' turnout was better – every single horse was immaculately turned out. So it is swings and roundabouts!'

Rider classes

Australia also has many rider or 'equitation' classes; these are virtually unheard of in the UK, especially at the higher levels. The rider is judged for his seat, his ability to control and manage the horse, his position and overall appearance. At the beginning of January 1995, the first Rider of the Year Show was held by the Victorian EFA (see page 158), and was very well supported by competitors. At the Royal and most other shows, rider classes are held for the under 8s; 8s and under 12s; 12s and under 16s; 16s and under 21s; and 21s and over. Champions are chosen from the winners and the reserves of these classes. Workouts are either set by the organizers, or can be made up by the riders as long as they incorporate certain

• THE CHANGING SHOW SCENE •

Australia's Maureen Walker has seen some great changes in the Australian show horse industry during her career: 'It has become much larger, and as a result of this, competitors are tending to specialize more, perhaps in one breed or in the hacking – ridden showing – category. A few years ago it was possible to attend an agricultural show and compete in all the events: led, or in-hand classes; hacking; jumping and event sporting – that is, competitions which include tent pegging and novelty contests such as pole bending – and also campdrafting, a uniquely Australian sport in which a horse has to field a cow around obstacles, possibly the Australian version of the USA's barrel racing. However, the programmes are now too packed for this, with classes needing to be completed in a limited time frame, so all competitors can do nowadays is to specialize in hacking or led classes, or jumping, for example.'

Maureen believes that the major strengths of the Australian show horse are its beauty, elegance and high standard of training: 'The Australian show horse has a great beauty and elegance, whether a small 12hh pony or a large hack over 16hh. It is very well educated, and emphasis is also made on movement and accuracy; this is possibly because most show riders also do dressage, at some time or other.'

requirements. Rider classes appear to be gaining in prestige. Competitors in senior rider classes are usually highly respected members of the show community, who teach students and train horses; accordingly, more and more young show riders aspire to win champion rider classes.

AN AUSTRALIAN PERSPECTIVE

by Kate Ames

The Australian show industry is one of the most solid and active in the Australian equestrian world, with shows being held throughout the country every weekend; the show horse industry thrives, and the hacking (ie showing) community is very strong – members enjoy a sport which continues to grow in numbers and quality in both the ridden and led sphere. The quality of ponies and hacks, and the standard of riding by competitors have both improved dramatically over the years.

Australia is a large country, approximately the same size as the USA, but with only seventeen million people and seven major centres around which the population is concentrated; this in itself sets the scene for the Australian equestrian arena as a whole. The Equestrian Federation of Australia (the EFA) is responsible for the administration of equestrian sports in Australia; it has only recently been made a constitutional federation, representing each state of Australia within a national committee. Each state has an autonomous EFA branch, and whilst they operate very independently of one another, they are still responsible to the federal body, based in the state of South Australia.

The EFAs in each state have, until recently, been the sole organizers of the major hacking (showing) events in each state. However, due to discontent within the hacking communities in the states of New South Wales, Queensland, Western Australia and now South Australia, alternative associations have been set up to administer and organize major events. The main reason for this was that it was felt that the EFA concentrated mainly on the 'Olympic discipline' sports of dressage, showjumping and eventing, and that the fees paid by the hacking community, which were as high as those paid by other members of the EFA, were not seen in their return to the hacking industry.

Due to this dissatisfaction, some states have seen the growth of hack councils, which are popular and

(Above) The three various ways of showing ridden Arabians (from left to right): Western, English and costume (traditional) (Catherine Witham)
(Right) New York and Roy Davis dominated the hack classes in Australia in 1994 (Kate Ames)

well organized and represent the show horse community – although as most competitors who are not involved in the politics of it all admit, this development only serves to provide more avenues of competition. In Tasmania, however, competitors must be members of the EFA to be able to compete in Royal Agricultural Shows, and in this particular state, the issue of hack councils has not arisen. In Victoria, to be eligible for the Royal Melbourne Show, horses must be registered with a recognized society: a breed society or the EFA (Victoria branch).

The hack councils have been extraordinarily successful. The Hack Council of New South Wales was the first to be established. Originally set up in 1982 as the Hack Exhibitors' Association of NSW, it became aligned with the EFA in 1985. In 1991, the organization again became autonomous, and the NSW Hack Council was formed. This was shortly followed by the Hack Council of Queensland and the Hack Council of Western Australia, both in 1993. The councils run their own shows for those not affiliated with the EFA, and the highlight is the Grand National Horse of the Year Show, for ridden horses only, held in April of each year in New South Wales. Many members of the hacking community are, however, still members of the EFA.

Avenues for Australian showing (hacking)

There are two major avenues for showing throughout the year. Agricultural shows culminate in a Royal Show in each state capital; in Tasmania and the Northern Territory there are two shows per year. Competitors must qualify at local shows, and Royal Shows also provide many led and halter classes for breed showing. Sydney and Melbourne Royal Shows are probably the biggest in the country in terms of prestige, although Brisbane is the largest in terms of numbers. Brisbane is the capital of Queensland, a state which has a long and very strong agricultural tradition.

A National Horse of the Year Show is held at the end of each year by the EFA, and this has in the past rotated between states. The current home for this show is Victoria, where it will stay until the year 1999. Eligible are the horses which have won champion titles at the various EFA State Branch

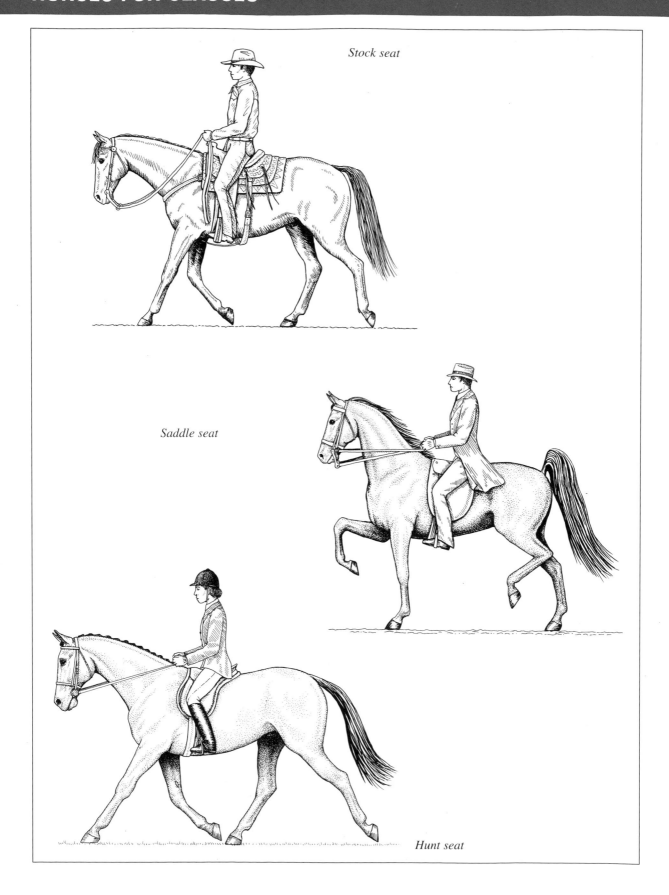

Stock seat

Saddle seat

Hunt seat

Horse of the Year Shows throughout the year.

Most people involved in the industry feel that the developments have been successful. The development of the hack council has not only highlighted the potential inadequacies of the EFA, it has also served to promote the sport and its importance within the EFA and the general horse community, and has provided competitors with more opportunities for prizes and competition.

UNITED STATES OF AMERICA

In the United States, most horse shows are organized by the American Horse Shows Association (AHSA) whose regulations affect twenty-four groups of show horses, a range that touches upon almost all areas of modern horsemanship. The whole spectrum of showing in the USA is entirely different to either Australia or the UK. Ridden showing is divided into three types of 'seat': the Western (or stock) seat, the saddle seat and the hunter seat, and the breed of horse used is not relevant. These classes are therefore 'equitation' classes, and not true 'showing' classes as recognized in the UK. However, within the show classes themselves it is required that riders adopt one or other of these 'seats', so 'equitation' classes are linked to showing. The closest comparison you can make between ridden classes in the UK and the USA is to consider the 'types' of horse shown in what are known as 'performance' classes. For example, where in the UK hacks and cobs are shown, in the USA there are classes for the following:

Five- and Three-gaited American Saddlebred
These horses have two extra, innate gaits that make them special in the show world: the 'rack' and the 'slow gait'. The gaits are exceptionally smooth, and they are single-footed, each hoof touching the ground separately. Riders wear a thigh-length coat, jodhpurs and soft derby, and they ride in the saddle-seat style. A five-gaited horse is shown with a full mane and tail and in a full, or double bridle; a three-gaited horse has a roached (shaved) mane and may have a shaved or full tail.

Paso Fino The Paso Fino's abilities and gaits are unique, resulting in classes that are not duplicated or similar to any other breed. In competition, Paso Finos demonstrate the *paso corto*, the even-beated

walk with moderate forward speed and extension; and the *paso largo*, a gait with rapid forward movement and cadence. Pasos show at the walk, the canter and the 'lope' (a slow canter). Many of the classes are divided by the age and sex of the horse. Sections are for pleasure, trail, versatility, performance, equitation and costume.

Park Horse The park horse is the most elegant, animated and showy of the Arabian and Morgan horses which participate in these breed performance classes. Exhibits are shown at the walk, trot and canter, and are judged on their brilliance, presence and style – they must perform each gait with high knee and hock action. They are shown in a double bridle with full mane and tail. As with most performance divisions, classes are often sorted according to the age and status of rider or horse.

English Pleasure This is the closest we get to the UK's riding horse classes. The English pleasure horse performs with enthusiasm and animation, yet must be 'clearly a pleasure to ride'. English pleasure horses are shown at the strong or 'road' trot, the extended trot and the canter. Horses in this class do not have as notable knee and hock action as park horses, and move with moderate collection of stride. Horses are shown in a double bridle, with full mane and tail.

Country English Pleasure, Country Pleasure or **Classic Pleasure** Like the English pleasure horse, the country English pleasure horse demonstrates easy animated gaits with an emphasis on appearing to be a pleasure to ride. They, too, are often shown at the extended, or 'road' trot, and the hand gallop, in addition to the walk, trot and canter. A further test of their ridability is the requirement that they must halt, stand, and back up.

Hunter Pleasure This is the closest we get to the 'weight' show hunters in the UK. Especially popular in the Arabian and Morgan breeds, hunter pleasure horses are judged on their suitability to be a foxhunter. They move with a natural, long, free-flowing stride, and must appear to be pleasurable and calm to ride. They are shown at the walk, trot, canter and hand gallop, and may be asked to back up and stand quietly.

English Show Hack This category closely mirrors the UK hack class, except that it is exclusive to the Arabian breed. The English show hack shows to the judge its well mannered paces and quality, and

Shiflet ©

(Left) American Saddlebred: the five-gaited world's Grand Champion CH Man On The Town, ridden by George Knight, trots down victory lane for his owner Jean McLean of Harrodsburg, Kentucky (American Saddlebred Horse Association)

(Right) Western pleasure is judged 80 per cent on the performance of the horse, and only then on its condition and conformation. Avenue's Easter Flash, by Mucho Bueno Lynx out of Pawnees, and owned by Chris Sadler, is ridden here by Sheila Whelan in a Western pleasure class at Solihull Riding Club (GB) (Dianna M. Whelan)
(Below right) Western trail, judged on the performance of the horse over obstacles, with the emphasis on manners, response to the rider and attitude. Sheila Whelan on Joe Hawkeye, an experienced trail horse capable of mastering most trail obstacles with precision (Dianna M. Whelan)

'demonstrates complete and proper training of the show animal'. Horses are shown at the walk, trot and canter, and at the normal, collected and extended gaits, and they perform these gaits with complete control by the rider.

Mounted Native Costume In keeping with the rich tradition of the Arabian, the mounted native costume class is a showcase for the dress and styles of the Bedouin culture. Flowing capes, head-dresses, jewellery and ornamented bridles are favourite choices among entrants, who are often so numerous that the costume class is the most popular at Arabian shows.

Parade Horse Parade horses are exceptionally eye-catching animals that radiate personality and flash. They perform at the animated walk and the parade gait, a true, high-prancing movement that should not exceed 5 miles (8km) per hour. Competitors must often parade gait over a fifty-foot (15m) section of ground, and should they complete it in less than seven seconds, they are penalized. Parade horses are shown in a stock (Western) saddle with silver or Mexican ornamentation. Riders wear outfits reminiscent of the Old West, including cowboy boots and hat. Spurs and guns are optional. Horses are shown with a long mane and full tail. Classes are divided by colour of the horse and by the status of the rider. Popular breeds in the parade division include the American Saddlebred and the Palomino, or often the Golden (Palomino) Saddlebred.

Western horses

The Western horse competes in many different forms, but usually specializes in one. These different categories are:

Western pleasure horse: Based on the tradition of the working cow horse, which needs to be a smooth, versatile ride over long days of working cattle, today's Western pleasure horse must exhibit and is judged on its tractable, obedient personality and slow, steady gaits that are comfortable for both horse and rider. Horses are shown at the walk, jog (slow trot), lope (slow canter) and hand gallop.
Reining or stock horse: Performs patterns, including spins, sliding stops, rundowns and

Avis '82

circles, demonstrating its versatility and rapport with the rider.

Working cow horse: Works a cow to specific criteria, such as holding the cow at one end of the pen, and then working it down the side of the arena while demonstrating several turns.

Trail Horse: Negotiates logs, water, small jumps, bridges and gates to show its partnership with its rider on the trail. Because of their versatility, trail horses are frequently shown in Western pleasure as well.

Almost all breeds participate in the Western divisions, especially Arabians and Morgans, and American Saddlebreds have also become a popular choice. Western horses are shown with long or shortened manes and full tails. Competitors ride in the stock seat style.

There are numerous breeds of horses and ponies that are extensively competed in the USA, with diverse talents and heritages. Some breeds are uniquely American, while others trace their ancestry over many centuries and throughout many continents. In-hand showing provides avenues for each of the breeds (see Chapter 9).

The American hunter scene

Shows for hunters are very popular in the United States, and classes range through nine different sections: green conformation; regular conformation; hunter breeding; green working; regular working; junior hunter; children's hunter; hunter pony; amateur owner hunter; adult amateur hunter.

For the first two years of showing, horses may be shown as 'green' (novice) hunters, after which they are required to move into the regular sections. The American show hunter of today is an elegant, mannerly, athletic performer; it must perform over a course of eight fences simulating obstacles found in the hunting field such as stone walls and coops,

and horses are judged on jumping style and their suitability to work as a foxhunter – this is similar to working hunter classes in the UK. The horse's jumping style and way of going are most important. The hunter pony, children's hunter and junior hunter classes are for those riders under eighteen years of age.

QUARTER HORSES IN THE UK

The Quarter Horse is the most popular and numerous breed of horse world-wide, and can be seen competing in all equestrian disciplines, from showing in English and Western style competition, to dressage, eventing, racing and even polo. Many Quarter Horse owners belong to the British Quarter Horse Association (BQHA) and to the American Quarter Horse Association (AQHA). In addition to participating in the traditional range of equestrian events in the UK, Quarter Horse owners also take part in various shows each year that are specific to the breed; these will include a number of classes, such as:

Western (USA and UK)	Western (USA only)	English
In-hand	Working Cow Horse	In-hand
Reining	Team Penning	Hunt Seat Equitation
Western Riding	Pole Bending	Jumping
Western Pleasure	Roping	Working Hunter
Trail	Cutting	Hunter/Hack
Showmanship		Hunter under Saddle
Western Horsemanship		
Barrel Racing		

In addition to English and Western classes offered by breed shows in the UK, Western shows are also organized by the Western Equestrian Society (WES) or by shows affiliated to them. Both types of show on the whole follow the rules set down by the AQHA.

American Saddlebreds excel under Western tack
(American Saddlebred Horse Association)

6

EQUIPMENT FOR THE JOB

CHOOSING THE CORRECT TACK

Bridles

For hunters, a double bridle with plain noseband and browband is correct and it should be of a heavier type of leather than is customarily used for a riding horse or hack. A pelham may also be used (with double reins), and is often seen in the cob classes. Four-year-old hunters are encouraged to be shown in a snaffle: 'It is better to have a horse going well in a snaffle than badly in a double, at this stage,' says Allister. Martingales are only permitted in working hunter classes.

Hunter foals are shown in a plain leather headcollar

• ALLISTER'S CHOICE OF BRIDLE •

'We do use pelhams,' says Allister, 'but always with two reins rather than a dividing rein, or a rounding. We use various pelhams and bits to suit individual horses, as long as they have got double reins. If a horse is not happy in a double bridle, but it goes beautifully in a pelham then there is no reason why it shouldn't go in a pelham. Four-year-olds can be shown in a snaffle. Similarly it is better to have a horse going nicely in a snaffle than badly in a double; although we do find that if a horse is happy and going well in a snaffle, it will nearly always go into a double bridle without any fuss. It is better to spend longer getting the horse going well in a snaffle than to try and get it in a double as soon as possible. Occasionally you do get a horse that just doesn't settle in a snaffle, and often in these cases a pelham is the answer.'

Hacks and riding horses both wear lighter-weight double bridles but with coloured or fancy browbands, as do children's show ponies. Novice show ponies are always expected to go in a snaffle, whereas for open show ponies a double bridle is required. For lead-reins and first ridden, a snaffle bridle is compulsory. For show hunter ponies and working hunter ponies, the tack used is similar to hunters, but obviously of a size and weight to suit the pony. Native breeds are shown in plain tack and although stitched browbands are acceptable, coloured or fancy ones are not.

'When choosing a suitable weight of bridle you have to consider the class and your horse's head,' says Allister. 'We show almost every hunter in a flat noseband and plain browband. The general rule is, the bigger the head the broader the bridle. We

Most horses shown in mainstream classes are exhibited in a double bridle, except novices which are shown in a snaffle

A good type of in-hand bridle. Note how the lead-rein is attached around the coupling and the noseband, in order to protect the horse's mouth if he prances about

When choosing a suitable weight for the bridle, you have to consider the class for which it is required, and your horse's head. This is a hunter brood mare

An in-hand hunter filly with perfectly matched bridle: an exquisite picture

A straight-cut saddle enhances the horse's shoulder, and allows greater ease of movement. Note also how a white numnah does not detract from a grey horse's outline

always use coloured browbands for riding horses and hacks. However, for riding horses they should be more sombre than for the hacks which can have very flashy browbands. The bridles also get narrower as you go down the scale, so they will be quite broad for the heavyweight hunters, less so for the lightweight, less still for the riding horses, and so on.'

Saddles

Allister stresses that a saddle which is comfortable for both you and the judge is most important. It should be straight cut, but can have a bit of knee roll if required. 'The picture has got to look right,' he says. 'It would be ill-advised to have a small saddle on a heavyweight horse, even if it feels good to you, because it would look ridiculous. You are allowed a numnah under the saddle, and we do use them because we feel it saves the horse's back and the saddle, but the numnah has to be totally

unobtrusive. It's no good putting a fluffy white numnah under a black saddle on a bay horse, because the contrasting effect is far too startling! You can get special numnahs to fit all shapes of saddles in all colours so there really is no excuse.'

Wendy continues: 'The straight-cut showing saddle is ideal, preferably with a full panel and knee roll as this will provide maximum comfort for the judge. For working hunters and working hunter ponies a more forward-cut saddle is acceptable because of the jumping involved, but most people will have only one saddle, so at a lesser level a general purpose saddle is acceptable. However, a straight-cut saddle does enhance the horse's shoulder and makes the overall picture better, so this is something to invest in if you want to go showing seriously.'

In Australia and the USA

Australian horses are shown in much the same tack as horses in the UK. Many horses in the USA are also shown in similar tack (although it is often far more highly decorated), except those shown in Western classes (see Chapter 5): in these, horses

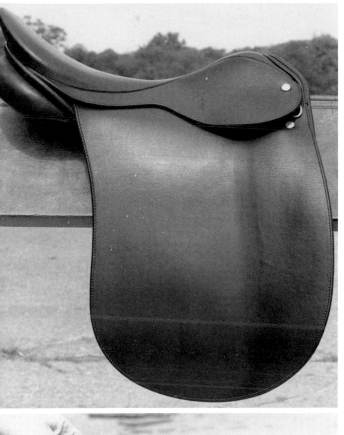

must be shown in either a snaffle, a standard Western curb bit, or a hackamore (bitless bridle), and a Western saddle. Riders must wear a Western hat, a long-sleeved shirt and tie, trousers, chaps and Western boots.

• SUE RAWDING'S PET HATES •

• Bridles that are far too thin and wispy; when I am judging I hate having to ride a horse in narrow reins. Even on a hack I like something reasonably substantial, but often horses are wearing little more than string-like bridles.
• I dislike seeing tight throatlashes, and there does seem to be a tendency for this in the ring.
• Curb chains secured in a strange fashion is also not an uncommon sight, and is really annoying.
• I loathe seeing spurs hanging off the heels of boots.
• Some saddles are horrendous to ride on; competitors should always give thought to the fact that the judge has to ride on the saddle too!
• Make sure that the leathers will go short or long enough for any judge, and that stirrup irons will accommodate small or large feet; have your groom bring in another pair if necessary.
• I like to see three-year-old in-hand show horses in double bridles.

CORRECT TURNOUT

The Rider's turnout

You want the horse to come into the ring and say 'look at me', but the impression he makes will be wasted if you look so shabby that all the judge can say is 'Oh yes, but just look at you!' If you detract from your horse's appearance in any way, you are failing him.

For mainstream showing the rider should wear a well cut tweed coat; canary, fawn or buff breeches (not white), and long boots; and the same applies

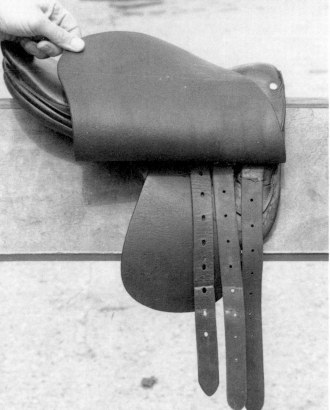

(Above) The straight-cut showing saddle is ideal, preferably with full panel and knee roll as this will provide maximum comfort for both you and the judge

(Left) Pony showing saddles often have only half panels

for riding horses. Women may wear a tweed, or plain blue or black coat. Any form of leather or string glove is acceptable. A collar and tie is usual, with the tie pinned down, with a plain malacca or leather cane and spurs completing the picture. However, each society does have its own rules, so always check these carefully.

In children's show pony classes navy jackets are worn; whereas for hunter ponies and working hunter ponies dress is the same as for adult mainstream showing, except that children should wear well fitting short jodhpur boots; although in 15hh pony classes they may wear longer boots.

Some shows stipulate that competitors must have safety hats; in this case a crash helmet with a dark, neatly fitting cover to match the coat is quite acceptable, or a deep-crown velvet hat with a safety harness up to current standard. Some people still prefer to wear the old-style hats without a harness, as they feel this creates a more attractive turnout.

For pony showing it is compulsory to wear a safety hat, as it is for the jumping phase of adult working hunters. The UK societies have not yet made it compulsory to wear safety helmets, but some individual shows do stipulate that they must be worn on the showground, so always check the schedule before setting out from home.

• ROBERT OLIVER ON TURNOUT •

Cleanliness of everything to do with both horse and rider – and not just on show days! – is a must. In the ring everything must be spotless, including polished boots and their soles! What you do outside the ring also counts. You always want to promote a professional attitude, so for example there is no need for dirty wellington boots or scruffy clothes when warming up: a show is a show from the minute you arrive until the horse is back home in his box.

Your horse's tack should be turned out nicely, and it must always be well looked after. Whatever the time of day or night, always hang it up properly; whether it is second-hand or brand new, it should be treated with respect. The newcomer can make do with second-hand and still be tops; I don't think I have ever bought a new saddle!

• ALLISTER'S TURNOUT •

Allister wears a tweed coat, but 'nothing too bright,' he says, 'just smart. Your colour and tie can be carefully chosen to complement the overall picture. For instance, if I am competing in a riding horse class I tend to wear a white and maroon stripe shirt with a white collar, and a yellow with burgundy spot tie, with the horse's browband to match it. For hacks I change the tie to a brighter one to match a hack's more flashy browband, and for hunters I wear a very pale yellow shirt with a green and yellow tie, which complements my jacket. To be visually pleasing is the key. Always wear a good pair of gloves – I wear a pair of hogskin gloves – not a knitted woolly pair! A brown leather-covered cane is fine; I myself would definitely avoid black gloves and black cane for adult competitions. Always wear long boots, and try to wear spurs, even if they are dummy ones, because they finish off the dress, and look better than no spurs at all. For final judging at Wembley, or at international shows, there is a totally different dress code – so check the rules with your particular society if you are lucky enough to reach this stage.'

Allister just before the preliminary judging at Wembley; he wears the same clothes as for general showing (except the bowler hat, of course!)

In Australia

The outfits for riders in Australia are beginning to show a slow trend towards more variation in riding coats, according to Caroline Wagner. As she explains: 'In the past there were a lot of dark colours – black, navy and grey; now we are seeing a gradual return to tweeds, and greens and browns, with the riding coats becoming shorter and not so full in the skirt. I personally feel these are good changes – tweeds and greens and so on tend to complement the natural tones in bays, browns and chestnuts.'

The overall turnout should be visually pleasing. This horse has a white browband in order to draw the judge's eye, as the horse itself has no white markings

Groom's turnout

Your attendant, or 'groom', should look respectfully tidy. A lot of the county shows insist that they wear a collar and tie, and a jacket and hat (*not* a head-scarf in the case of lady attendants). A groom is considered to be part of the rider's overall turnout, and this should be remembered at all times – and this includes their behaviour in the ring.

7

TRICKS OF THE TRADE

OPTIMIZING THE HORSE'S CONDITION

By the time the shows are well under way, your horse should be at his peak. He should still be nice and round and well conditioned, and proper strapping, coupled with sufficient exercise and good feeding will ensure his muscles are tight, not fat and flabby. It is also important to continue to assess his condition regularly, as travelling and the show environment can take its toll on some horses. Sometimes, however, you may feel your horse never really looks on top form, no matter how vigilant you are about looking after him; but this can often be attributed to faults in his make-up – slightly poor conformation can prevent a horse from thriving, as can an anxious type of temperament. Nevertheless, if you come up against such problems you should not despair, as there are many things you can do to make the best of what you have: you cannot make an ugly duckling into a swan, but it is possible to make a king out of a prince.

COMPLEMENTING A HORSE'S LOOKS

The most important thing on which to focus should be your horse's good points, not his bad. You are trying to show that because your horse has so much going for him, a few little 'niggly' faults here and there do not account for much. You have to enhance your horse, and not try to change him, for you can never do that.

Wendy explains further: 'If you have a horse that is a bit long in the back, you can use a saddle that is slightly longer in the seat, although it still wants to fit the horse properly. If the horse has not got the best of hocks you might want to cut the tail a little on the shorter side, so that it is in line with the hocks rather than below them; this has the

effect of drawing the eye away from the hocks themselves. You can also use the length of the tail to make the hind leg look slightly different – a tail shorter than normal has the effect of lengthening the leg, and a longer tail has the effect of shortening it to a small degree.'

Just before going into the ring at Wembley, Allister's small hack has his face shaved in order to present a smooth, streamlined finish

Cosmetics

Allister will use petroleum jelly around the eyes and muzzle in order to enhance the horse's facial features. 'We also blacken the feet, as opposed to just oiling them,' he says, 'and we use "blacker than black" on the hooves as it really does blacken the horse's feet for the whole duration of the show. We also chalk white legs, and may cover scars with a little boot polish of the correct colour for the horse if necessary. On a hack we will use more finishing touches than on a riding horse, but then

> **• DISGUISING FAULTS •**
>
> *According to John Rawding, if you use anything to disguise faults, scars or any blemishes you are cheating in the show ring. A good judge will know what you are trying to do, but it is only right to show the horse as naturally as possible. John has a particular memory of this sort of behaviour:*
>
> *'I once judged a class at Royal Norfolk, and when I ran my hand down a particular horse's leg I came away with black boot polish all over it! This would be enough to put a horse down, in my eyes. However, the problem is that such "cosmetics" don't stop at a bit of boot polish: a few years ago I was at a show with a good friend of mine who was a top show name then. He saw a pony walking round, and turned to his wife and said "That's my old pony!" She replied "Of course it's not, it's got a white star and your pony never had a star!" But he persisted, saying "That is him, I am absolutely sure of it!" He went up to the pony and touched the white star, and found that it had been "freeze-branded" on! It was, without a doubt, one and the same pony.'*
>
> *Wife Sue is emphatic about her own view: 'I like to see a horse turned out very correctly in the old-fashioned way, rather than one with gimmicks. I like to see nice "shark's teeth" brush marks, a really well pulled tail and nice neat plaits. I don't like to see things that a competitor has obviously tried to disguise, but I don't mind him trying to enhance a horse's good points – after all, they are already there. Things like white chalk on the legs and little Vaseline around the eyes and nose are fine in my book.'*

not so many for a hunter. Our hacks have quarter marks and shark's teeth; the riding horses and hunters have only the shark's teeth.'

Wendy uses 'Brilliantine' around a horse's nose to make the muzzle dark, and may use stage make-up of a colour to suit each horse's coat, to cover up scars and blemishes. 'One thing that does stand out on a horse, and especially on steel greys, are pink areas on the face where there in no skin pigment. You can use eyeshadow of the right shade around these – the cream variety, not the powder – but be careful to blend it in well.'

Tack Tips

'If you have a horse with a plain head, it is better to have a nice wide browband and noseband, in fact a chunkier type of bridle altogether to cover the head up, or at least break it up,' says Allister. 'Also, whatever tack you use must be spotless – dirty tack does nothing to enhance a horse's appearance, and only signifies a shabby attitude.'

COMPLEMENTING A RIDER'S SHAPE

The way the rider's clothes are cut is also important and can hide a multitude of sins. There is nothing worse than having a jacket which is too tight or too big; it looks messy and does not create the right impression, so always ensure you are turned out tidily. There may not be any need to buy a new outfit if finances are tight, as many saddlers do a good trade in used showing wear; so there really is no excuse for looking as if you have just borrowed someone else's outfit.

DEVELOPING A ROUTINE

In order to avoid last-minute hitches, it is important to allow plenty of time, both for preparation and on the day of the show. Here are a few tips:

• Leave yourself extra travelling time in case of bad traffic or a breakdown.
• Get everything ready for the show the night before, because showing usually involves early starts.
• Make sure you have got water and a haynet, and everything your horse might need to keep comfortable, as well as the equipment you will need to show with.

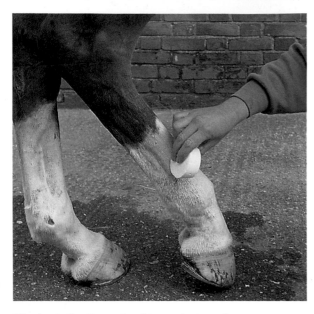

Wendy chalks George's white socks in order to brighten them

Showing involves many early mornings. Wendy starts up the lorry, wishing she were still in bed!

(Right) Getting to the show early means you can allow your horse to have a leisurely look round the showground, or time to relax on the box before any preparations begin. Wendy takes Josh's pony for a jolly

---

Some shows send out passes and numbers before the day, so either remember to take them with you, or collect them as soon as you get there; then find out where your rings are.

• If you haven't got a specific time for your class, find out how the previous classes are running and generally get everything sorted out, so that you are calm and know where you should be and when.

Dealing with show days

The Hoods have an established routine on show days, which Allister describes:

'It is important to be prepared for your show well in advance – if you have forgotten anything you can't nip back home to collect it. We double up with equipment and leave it permanently in the lorry, so that things such as grooming kits and plaiting materials are always in there.

'We get up early at home to plait and bandage the horses, so that once at the show they can relax without us fussing around them. We also try to keep their feed times constant, so for example if we have to get up at 2am to get on the road, we don't instantly feed them – they may not get fed until they get to the show, which will coincide with their normal routine. Getting to the show early in the morning is important as it allows the horses time to relax on the lorry, when the showground is not too busy; then by the time it does start to liven up they are already acclimatized to the atmosphere. If you arrive late, your horse has to cope immediately with a busy atmosphere, coupled with you trying to get him ready and then straight off the lorry into the ring. This is unfair on the horse, and will not see continued success.

'If you arrive early you can do exactly as you please. Your horse may benefit from having half an hour on the lunge before being brought back into the lorry to have his breakfast; or give him a walk round the collecting ring while it is still fairly empty. Being early means that you can make the best of the show day, at a pace that suits your horse.'

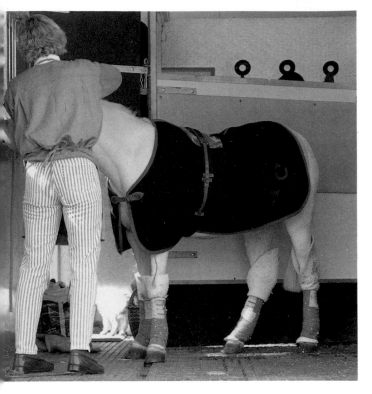

Arriving early at a show means you have plenty of time to prepare your horse without rushing him, or yourself. Wendy puts some finishing touches to Josh's pony

'Always keep an eye on your classes,' says Allister. 'Some shows do print a start time in the catalogue, but this can be subject to change. If there are fewer horses forward in the classes that precede yours you could be called far earlier than you expected, so be prepared for this. Similarly, if classes are running late you don't want to have your horse in the collecting ring waiting about for hours.'

PREVENTIVE MEASURES WHEN TRAVELLING THE SHOW HORSE

Allister's horses always have bandages and tail guards put on, but because his lorry is well padded they do not need poll guards. With a mucky horse, the tail is bandaged all the way down to prevent it from becoming stained with dung. On arrival at the show this should be taken off, however, otherwise

As Allister has described, the Hoods never plait the night before. If they have to start early, haynets are put in the lorry for the journey, and the horses will be given their breakfast at the showground at their normal feed time. Such an early routine also gives you plenty of time to collect your numbers, and to see where all the rings and also the collecting rings are. When it is time for your first class, the horse should be prepared quietly for the ring; he should not be rushed into a flap. All your actions will be transmitted to the horse, so if you are excited and nervous, rushing here and there and screeching at the top of your voice, how can you expect your horse to remain calm?

> ### • ROBERT OLIVER'S TOP TIP •
> *You must always remember that showing is supposed to be an enjoyable activity – if you don't have fun, there really is no point in doing it.*

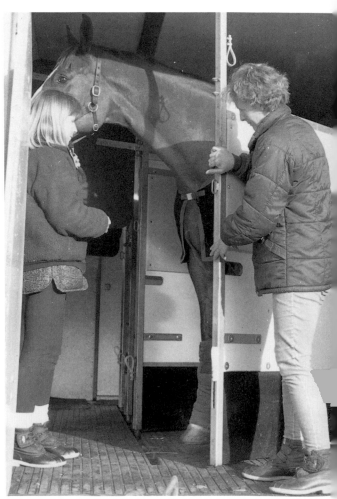

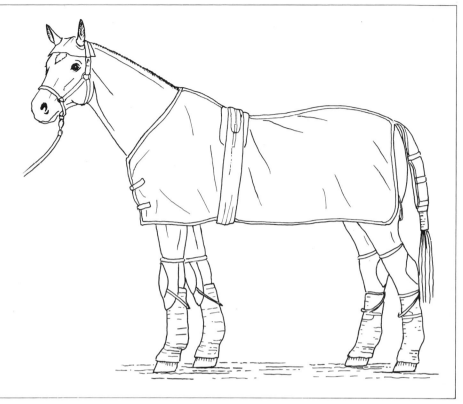

A horse dressed correctly and safely for travelling; he is well rugged up, and is wearing a poll guard to protect his head, knee and hock boots, leg bandages, and tail bandages and guard

the tail will not be full and flowing in the ring but will look like a piece of rope, all clamped together; just an ordinary tail bandage should be put on to keep the pulled part lying flat and neat. If your horse tends to become somewhat upset and warm when travelling, take care not to over-rug him, but just put on a cooler; and avoid the string type of sweat rug as these leave an imprint, and you can end up with a chestnut looking dappled! Other horses need more rugs because they become cold – don't forget, even in the height of summer in the UK, it can still be very chilly from around three to five in the morning when you are probably travelling.

One last point on travelling: you must take care not to drive too fast, even if the roads are deserted and especially if you arc not used to it. Always try and give your horse a comfortable, stress-free ride, and he will arrive at the show cool and relaxed. There is nothing worse than having to try and clean a sticky, sweaty horse just before his class.

(Left) Make sure the lorry partitions are spaced correctly for your horse. If they are not, he will not travel well and may arrive sweating and tucked up

• A MAN'S WORLD •

Showing is often considered to be a man's world, so what do the UK's most successful showing sisters feel about being 'women in a man's world'? Neither of the Hennessy sisters really give much thought to this eventuality:

'We started off our competitive lives on ponies,' says Sally, 'doing everything from gymkhana and showjumping to eventing, hunting and showing. Later on, both of us did a bit of point-to-pointing and BHS eventing, and there was always plenty of hunting and racing – Moggy even came a short-head second in the Newmarket Town Plate, the oldest amateur flat race on the calendar, so we have always competed against the men and thought nothing of it! When it came to showing it did seem a bit strange that the most successful people were men, but much of that you can put down to the fact that they have been doing it for a long time! In our job, you have to "give as good as you get" – neither Moggy nor I put up with much flack, and just get on with the job!'

8

RINGCRAFT

To Allister, ringcraft means being aware of what is going on at all times. This means knowing not only *where* the judge is watching, but *when* he is watching you, without having to look directly at him. You must also be aware of what everyone else in the ring is doing, including stewards and other competitors. It is something you have got to experience, but as long as you keep your wits about you, things should not get too tense. The more you compete, the easier it becomes, and the more experienced you become, the more quickly you react to what is happening all around you.

There is also a sort of unwritten 'code of conduct' for correct behaviour at showgrounds, a kind of 'showground etiquette' whereby competitors respect the need to refrain from monopolizing common facilities, such as the warm-up areas; to be organized so that the minimum inconvenience is caused to organizers and other competitors; but most of all that every participant is a good sportsman or woman.

'The idea,' says Wendy, 'is to create a frame around yourself, so that when the judge looks at your horse, there is neither another horse's rump in the picture in front of you nor another horse's head in the frame behind you. This may appear easy to achieve, but it is extremely difficult. It requires a lot of experience, practice and a great deal of concentration. You can learn a lot by watching other people, and can get help from professionals, but experience is the most important thing. So getting in the ring and doing it is the best preparation.'

• WHAT IS RINGCRAFT? •

Ringcraft means different things to different people. To Moggy and Sally Hennessy, it is knowing how to catch the judge's eye, even in the most crowded of rings. 'It is getting yourself into "that space"; getting the horse to look and go its best; standing it up properly in-hand; covering up those little faults as best you can and, hopefully, getting rewarded for your efforts!'

WHO CAN HELP?

Once you are at a show there are few people who can help you; your horse must have been well prepared beforehand, and you should have done all you can to know where you should be and when. However, it does help to have an assistant who can

Ringcraft means being aware of what is going on at all times. Face the Music takes little notice of distractions, but Allister is acutely aware of what is happening all around

keep an eye on whether classes are running to time or not, as well as one who can help with those last-minute checks to the girth and the rider's attire. Only you will know how your horse feels, and only you can manage him accordingly. It is pointless to try and copy someone else's tactics at this point, as your horse may be very different from theirs. The most sensible advice is to try and treat it like any other day: ride your horse as you always do at home, giving due consideration to his character and anticipating his reactions; this is the best you can do, so then just try to enjoy yourself. And if you can adopt this carefree attitude, you are more likely to be relaxed and smiling, which actually creates exactly the right impression in the ring. Don't worry about your position as this will only make you tense, just ride as it comes naturally. If your horse does do something wrong, then it is simply something you will have to put down to experience. Allister is always under quite a lot of pressure when he competes, as obviously his owners want him to do well. However, he has the mark of a true professional in that it all appears to be so easy. In fact some of the horses he rides are far from easy, yet they perform because of the discipline that Anne and Allister instil at home. But at the end of the day, showing is supposed to be a pleasurable activity, and all those involved should always bear this in mind.

• ROBERT OLIVER ON INSTRUCTION •
These days there are some super teachers, so get all the help you can afford. Whether it's part-time, full-time or in a clinic, it's surprising what valuable advice you can pick up.

WARMING UP

Knowing your own horse is of first importance when considering the best way to warm up. Second, knowing the layout and site of the warm-up area and collecting rings at various shows will help you to plan when to bring your horse up to the ring. If you are at a little local show where to warm up there is only a small, roped-off area which also serves as a collecting ring, and the secretary holds fort in a caravan, you are probably not going to need to work your horse in for as long as if you go

to a county show that has loud speakers, other agricultural animals, spectators and all the paraphernalia of a big event. You cannot expect your horse to behave in the same way at a small, quiet show as it does at a noisy, busy county show, so this must be taken into account when planning how to warm up.

'I often end up going off to find a quiet spot at the corner of the showground,' says Wendy, 'especially if the horse is young, or particularly nervous or a newcomer to shows.' At some shows, however, the only available space is the collecting ring, so you have just got to get on with it. It may help if you can get to the show early in the morning, as some horses will benefit from a warm-up early on, and then another short one as the showground becomes busier. If only a small area is available for warming up, try to stay on the inside of the track if you are just walking, allowing those going at a faster pace to do so uninterrupted. In addition, try to avoid cutting across anyone who is working on a circle at one end of the ring. Also remember that the collecting ring is solely for horses that will shortly be competing in a class; it is not an area for lungeing a fresh horse, or giving a lesson to a nervous rider.

When passing other riders in the collecting ring, bear in mind the 'school rule' of left shoulder to left shoulder; this will help everyone and cause fewer 'near misses' or actual collisions. Also, warm-up time should not be used to tire the horse out before he goes into the ring; if your horse is very excited then the collecting ring is the last place you want to start any serious hard work. 'If we know we have a horse that is likely to be a little bit excitable, then it is worked very hard the day before the show,' explains Allister. 'As it becomes more experienced it may quieten down, but to avoid trouble we do work all our horses hard the day before a show.' Always remember, once you are at the show it is too late: shows are won at home.

Plan out your warm-up in advance. As with schooling, unless you have certain aims in view, the warm-up can become haphazard and this may be more unsettling to your horse. Aim to work him evenly on both reins, going through the paces of walk, trot and canter, trying to achieve a nice steady rhythm rather than perfectly formed movements. Once he has done enough and appears

relaxed, then take him off for a walk around before the class begins. Do not continue warming up to the point where he becomes bored, or gets hot and excited; he does not want to be sweating when he is in the show ring, so bear this in mind if he does sweat easily.

While you are in the collecting ring, keep a check on whether classes are running on time, and always be ready to enter the ring when your class is called, whether this is earlier or later than stated in the schedule. If you are late for your class the judge is entitled to refuse you entry, although an apology and explanation to the steward will probably allow you in without risk of compromising your horse being judged fairly. The lorry breaking down en route is a good excuse, over-sleeping is not!

'YOU'RE ON!'

Once you enter the ring you must concentrate fully on the job in hand. If you begin to look into the crowds you will become distracted, and may fail to anticipate any unwelcome moves by your horse.

Always ensure that you make enough space available in front of you to avoid cutting up other competitors when galloping past the judge

The important thing to remember is that you must keep your distance from horses both in front of and behind you. It is quite common to see a whole bunch of horses all together at one end of the ring, with only a couple enjoying a vast space at the other. Both Allister and Wendy are quick to anticipate trouble ahead. For example, if they see a group of horses in front, about to pass the judge and all bunched closely together, they will turn a circle in order to give themselves space – and this is important, because as you pass the judge you want your horse to be the only one he is looking at.

'A lot of people forget that there may be a great deal of empty space behind them,' says Allister. 'If you are aware that the pace you are travelling will cause you to catch up with the group of horses in front of you by the time you are passing the judge, then simply slow the pace while going around the back of the arena and make the corners a little deeper. This will provide those few extra seconds to set you apart from others. This is far better than constantly turning circles, and in many cases will avoid having to turn a circle altogether. If you do too many circles this will break the horse's rhythm and upset him, so always be aware of what is, or is not, going on behind you. Where horses are constantly turned in circles to avoid a crowd they have been known to associate this with "required" behaviour, and are then most surprised to find their rider trying to prevent them from doing so, when they take it into their own heads to turn circles!

'It is extremely bad manners to overtake another horse when in front of the judge. You will be totally obscuring the other horse from the judge's view, and while you may feel this to be advantageous, it is you the judge will mark down, not the horse he missed.'

. MAKING THE BEST OF IT .
'If I had to sum up in a sentence what ringcraft means to me,' says Sue Rawding, 'I would say "it means getting away with what you can"! It is up to each individual to know what his or her horse's best assets and paces are, and so make the best of those, possibly trying to cover up the not-so-good ones. For instance, it is not that difficult to disguise a bad gallop.'

'The thing is,' says John, 'you have got to do your homework before you go in the ring. You have got to have your horse spot-on before you go in.'

REQUIREMENTS IN THE RING

From the minute your horse enters the show ring he is being judged. Even if it appears that the judge is not watching you, you should assume that he is. 'You are always trying to present the horse to its very best advantage while it strides down in front of the judge,' says Allister, 'but if possible you want to establish a good rhythm and stick with it all the way around the ring. If you have got any adjustments to make you certainly do not want to be doing them in front of the judge. Hopefully you will not need to make many adjustments, but obviously things do not always run smoothly. Always anticipate your horse's moves and prepare for him to be spot-on as he makes the turn for the

(Top right) Allister has Regal Max spot-on at the turn just before coming down in front of the judge

(Right) That 'look at me' quality is the one that wins classes. Champion Hunter at Royal Norfolk 1994, Mrs J. Hutchinson's Smallprint, ridden by Peter Richmond

(Below) Things do not always go according to plan, but the mark of a good showman/woman is that he or she always looks relaxed

straight side of the arena which the judge is observing. You can overdo it though, so try not to fiddle with your horse for the sake of perfection, as this will cause tension and possibly undesirable results. Always keep half an eye on the judge, and take the opportunity to make any corrections at the point where he is bound to be looking away from you. You are always on show to the spectators, but what the judge does not see cannot be marked down.'

Everyone always wants to do their best while in the show ring; if they did not, then they would not be competing, but it can often cause both novice and experienced competitors to try too hard. 'The most important quality of the show exhibitor in the ring is to be able to assume an air of calmness,

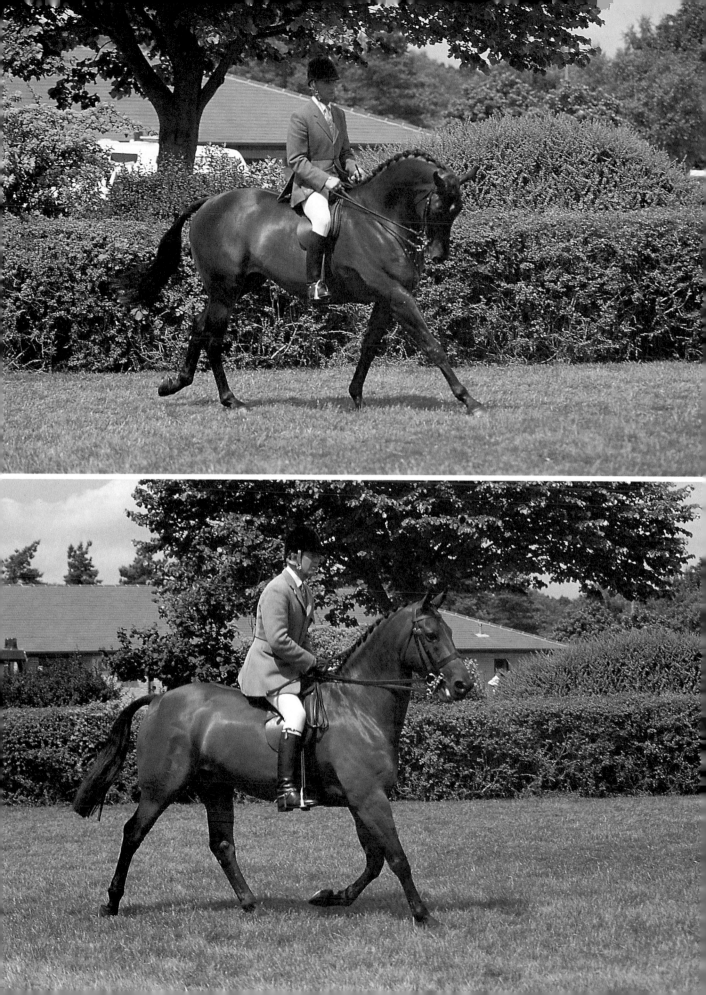

even if everything is going wrong,' says Allister. 'However, I do like a show horse that sits up and says "Look at me – I'm going somewhere!" Some horses can be relaxed to the point that they lose their presence, so it is a fine line between relaxation and sharpness. I'd rather see a horse that was just on the edge of that line, than one that was plodding around monotonously, as this creates a dull picture.'

For those who are new to showing, going into the ring for the first time may be a little daunting. You do not know what to expect, which may possibly make you feel a little inadequate. The order of events can alter, depending on the number of judges and their personal preferences; sometimes there may be one judge for conformation and another for the ride, for example. However, most classes do conform to a simple pattern.

IN-HAND CLASSES

• On entering the ring you will be directed by the steward to walk around the edge, usually on the right rein.
• You may then be asked to trot on.
• A change of rein, and a repeat of the preceding two paces usually occurs.
• The judge will then pull the class into a preliminary line-up; this may be in order of his initial preference, or it may simply be a random line-up.

A common signal from the steward to call you into line

Master showman John Rawding keeps one eye on the judge in order that he does not miss being called in

• Each horse will be pulled out in front of the judge to be assessed for conformation, and this is where your training of the horse to stand up correctly really counts. The judge may ask you a few questions about your horse's age, or breeding. Answer them truthfully, but do not elaborate – there is not the time, and he will not be swayed by statements such as, 'He won at Essex last week, you know'.
• The judge will then ask for the horse to be walked away from him and trotted back past him. When you turn to trot back, always remember to turn your horse away from you to the right. A good tip is to keep on trotting around the corner and down the back line; this shows he is willing, and provides the opportunity of encouraging him to lengthen his stride. If the judge likes your horse he will still have his eye on him, and such actions could see you moved up the line a few places.
• Once each horse has been assessed, the steward will ask the line to walk around the ring again. The judge will be summing up here, and if he has not

done so already will be picking his winner, so make sure your horse is alert and active.

• The steward will then call you in, so always be aware of what he is doing. It is not uncommon for someone to miss being called, and the horse below quickly stepping into his place unnoticed.

• The rosettes will be awarded, and a lap of honour for the winner/s will commence.

RIDDEN CLASSES

• On entering the ring you will be directed to walk around the outside.

• You will then be asked to trot and canter.

• The rein will be changed and the process repeated.

• You may also be requested to gallop on each rein, but often the gallop is performed on one rein only.

• You will then be called into line, usually in the judge's initial order of preference.

• If the class requires an individual show, you will then be asked to do this, in turn.

• The judge may then ride each horse.

Wendy 'presents' Melford Cornish Gold for the conformation inspection. Both horse and rider portray an air of tranquillity

• After the judge has ridden each horse, it is stripped in preparation for conformation assessment and ready for trotting up. Where there is both a ridden judge and a conformation judge, these two phases will take place simultaneously.

• You will be asked to walk around the outside of the ring once more while the judge considers his verdict.

• You will be called into line and awarded your rosette.

• A lap of honour follows, usually with the winner completing an extra circuit on his own.

SHOWMANSHIP

Either you have a flair for showmanship, or you do not. A lot can be learned by watching and listening to the top professionals, but at the end of the day you have got to have a 'feel' for showing, coupled with a real desire to want to do it. Showmanship is also about knowing exactly what will happen next, and preparing for it. *Be ready* before the steward calls you out. *Be prepared* to trot your horse up before the judge asks you to, and so on. Above all, *always* be prepared to *learn*.

The less experienced competitor is often let down by his apparent inability to carry out simple instructions. For example, if the judge asks you to do a short programme (say, in a riding horse class)

Allister trots up Face the Music in front of the judge; note how relaxed the horse seems

then this is what he wants, and a short, simple programme which shows all the paces on each rein is usually far more acceptable to him than one which includes flying changes and half passes. If he had wanted to assess a dressage test, then he would have chosen that discipline! Also, it is never advisable in a ridden class to tell the judge how to ride your horse. A tactful comment on some small point may be appreciated, but if you have to start making excuses for your horse then he probably should not be in the show ring.

The mark of a good showperson is that nothing *appears* to rile him or her, even if his two-thousand-pound stud fee foal has just come last behind a donkey! There is always another day, another show and another judge – so keep smiling. The three things any good showperson will always bear in mind are:

(Left) While manners are important, the horse must be allowed to relax when simply standing in the line-up awaiting his turn

(Below) Face the Music waits patiently for the judge to come and ride him

*The ultimate showman. Allister certainly had that
'showing flair', even in his earlier years. Here we see
Brown Buzzard, owned by the late Mr Thomas Hunnable,
Champion Hack at both the Royal International and the
Horse of the Year Show in 1981*

• Never throw in the towel if at first you arc at the
bottom of the line. Remember that everything can
change because of the way in which other horses
behave.

• Always pay particular attention to a horse's
manners while in the ring; good manners can often
put your horse above one of similar or even better
quality, but which behaves less well.

• Always be prepared for the next move.

Should you happen to know the judge, do not be
familiar with him, but treat him with the same
respect you show to any other official. Being chatty
with the judge will not only embarrass him, it will
also cause ill-feeling amongst other competitors.
The result is that however well earned your final
placing may be, the word 'fix' will be tripping off
their tongues, and this reflects badly on all
concerned.

What showmanship is *not* about, is leaving the
ring before the rosettes are handed out because you
are disappointed with your placing and want the
judge to know so. This is nothing more than an
immature display of bad manners. Any competitor
is within his or her rights to ask the judge about his
decision, but this should be in an amicable way and
because you intend to improve in the future.
However, if you have genuine complaints, these

should be taken up with the show organizers, and *not* with the judge in the ring.

In the United States there are actually classes for 'showmanship'. These are judged solely on the ability and effectiveness of the handler, together with the horse's turnout, rather than on the quality of the horse. The four main areas considered by the judge in such classes are:

• **Cleanliness:** This includes all aspects of clipping and turnout.
• **The handler's position:** This is quite a complex subject and involves far more than is required for in-hand classes in the UK. First, the handler should be in the correct position, that is between the horse's eye and shoulder while the horse is in motion. Then the handler should hold the lead-rein (shank) at the correct level and use it appropriately; also the hands should be carried in an effective, but natural way – and so on. So if you think showing horses in-hand in the UK is difficult – think again!
• **Performance of pattern:** This is the accomplishment of a set of manoeuvres dictated by the judge. While there is a standard individual pattern, judges are encouraged to detract from this in order to be challenging and so separate the wheat from the chaff.
• **Overall impression:** This includes everything and anything that happens in the ring, and even takes into account the handler's mannerisms!

Each breed and association in the US has its own set of rules for Western showmanship, and the responsibility for knowing them lies entirely with the competitor; so always check the appropriate exhibitor's guidelines for the relevant association. There are also English showmanship classes held in the US; these are fairly similar to those held in the UK.

THE OPPOSITION

Allister feels that the purpose of studying 'the opposition' is to try and make your horse better than them, and his advice is always to make the very best of what you have got. 'It is no good thinking that "so-and-so's here with a far better horse than mine, so it is pointless bothering today" because so-and-so's horse might explode in front of the judge, and if you are not trying to the best of

your ability, then you cannot take advantage of the situation. If, on the other hand, you are presenting the picture that says "Look at my horse, he is just as good as so-and-so's horse really," then you will have the best opportunity of the judge giving you a second look.' This is where showing is such a unique activity. If you are showjumping, you know whether you have got a clear round or not, but with showing nothing is cut and dried until the judge gives his verdict. Wendy's motto is 'never be defeatist'. There are many aspects to showing, so where your horse may fall down on one of them, he may pick up points on others.

Always be gracious to the opposition: congratulate them when they win and accept praise yourself with the goodwill intended. Above all though, praise your horse for allowing you to show him, whether you win or lose. We must never lose sight of the fact that horses are not machines, and in an unnatural environment such as the show ring we must be thankful that they are such amenable and willing creatures. An appalling practice seen at some shows is for certain competitors to attempt to relieve the frustration of losing by taking the horse back into the warm-up area to give him another hour's work in order to 'sort him out'. While a horse may have exhibited wilful behaviour in the ring when asked to perform in a way that he has done hundreds of times before, always remember how *you* feel on an off-day. School him at home if you must, but sleep on it first so that at least the horse has had the benefit of the doubt.

THE LINE-UP

Having been pulled into line you want to have your horse standing still. Allister allows his horses to relax in the line, but still has them attentive to what is going on. 'You will start to upset your horse if you keep him to attention all the time,' says Allister. A horse has got to be happy and relaxed while in the line-up, or else it will start to fidget, and this can have a knock-on effect, something

Never become too familiar with the judge; but no judge will resent your asking a question in the hope that you may be able to try and improve your performance. Wendy always tries to make time to say a few words to each competitor whenever she is invited to be a judge, as in this case during a hack class

which becomes only too apparent at smaller shows. Thus a less experienced rider may try to keep his or her horse looking 'perfect' all the time, and then it starts to get fed up. So it starts to fidget, which sets the next horse off, and then the next one, and so on. At larger shows the reason why the horses in the line-up are more well behaved is not necessarily because they are so much more used to the sights and sounds of the showground, but because they are allowed their own 'personal space', and a measure of relaxation.

STRESS MANAGEMENT

Show horses, and especially those at the top of the profession, are frequently subjected to arduous schedules. They may be stabled in small stalls for the duration of long shows, and this contributes to a lifestyle which overall is essentially inconsistent. In addition, they are often exposed to all sorts of alien sights and sounds: traction engines booming; flags flapping; parades of horse guards; cows, sheep and even pigs (which most horses detest); clapping, or

cheering crowds, and so on – all of which is far removed from the paddock at home. Although horses differ greatly in their reactions to such things, it comes as no surprise that they do suffer stress while at shows. The level of stress experienced will reflect the way the horse reacts and behaves. A little stress can be a good thing as it keeps the horse attentive and 'on his toes', but if he cannot cope with the level of stress he feels he will be physically and mentally unable to perform. An unacceptable level of stress usually manifests itself as either depression or anxiety, and if the horse is not prepared sufficiently well for the stresses of showing, he will forget his training at home and revert to his natural instincts: to flee from anything frightening.

In order to cope with stress, the horse must be carefully acclimatized to the showing environment. At first this is just by allowing him to have a look around the edges of the show; then he can gradually be exposed to more and more of the hubbub, but without anything demanding being asked of him. The trouble with larger shows is that

The line-up of small hacks at Wembley 1994. Although there is a lot going on in front of them, the horses are all really well behaved

• VIN TOULSON ON RINGCRAFT •
When it comes to ringcraft Vin Toulson has some excellent words of advice:
- *Do not produce a horse at a large show before it is really ready.*
- *Do not over-show a horse.*
- *Always allow plenty of time so that you are at a show at least one hour before your class.*
- *Horses and ponies vary a great deal as to how much riding in they need. If you find that a horse does not need much riding in you can always put it back in the box and bring it out again shortly before its class.*
- *Do not 'niggle' extensively at a horse when riding in, but try to find somewhere where you can let it stride on for a short distance.*
- *In the ring try to get out on your own, away from other competitors, never get crowded in. Always ride close to the rails, right on the outside of the ring, and do not cut your corners, particularly the corner after you have galloped.*
- *When you gallop don't go straight from a canter to a gallop. Before the straight side where you are going to gallop, gradually increase speed round the end of the ring so that you are already galloping down the straight side before you pass the judge, then gradually start to slow down before the next bend.*
- *If you are riding a horse that is inclined to get keyed up, relax yourself. If you are keyed up it communicates to the horse.*
- *If you are pulled in top, but then get put down, smile and congratulate the winners.*

a horse may be confined to his stall for hours on end while it is the turn of other horses to compete; and while exercising him in the warm-up areas is an important physical relief, it may not ease the psychological stress he feels. It is therefore very beneficial to walk him out in-hand around the showground, as this allows him to relax and unwind, without feeling that he has to 'work', and gives him the chance to view the scene at his leisure.

Another problem may arise from the horses stabled on each side, as these may cause your horse to feel threatened. If finances allow you could also rent the stable next door to use as a tack and feed store; this will help your horse to feel he has his own space. Some horses also appreciate having blinds put up between neighbouring boxes and for a period of time at the front of their box. If you make this a common practice while at shows, say for three hours every afternoon, your horse will soon begin to realize that as soon as the blinds go up he can let his defences down and enjoy an uninterrupted rest.

9

BREED AND IN-HAND SHOWING

HUNTER BREEDING

Affiliated in-hand classes come under the jurisdiction of the National Light Horse Breeding Society, in the same way as ridden classes, and judges will be selected from the hunter breeding panel. Classes are held for hunter brood mares with their own foal at foot; for hunter foals, that is, a colt, gelding or filly foaled in the current year of showing; for hunter yearlings, two-year-olds and three-year-olds. The major shows do have separate classes for fillies and geldings, but the NLHBS does not insist that all shows do because of the limited number of entries they receive. Some shows will divide classes if more than a certain number of entries are forward on the day. Classes are also held for small youngstock, that is, horses estimated not to reach over 15.2hh at maturity.

HACK BREEDING

All hack breeding classes at affiliated shows are qualifiers for the In-Hand Hack of the Year Championships at the British Show Hack, Cob and Riding Horse Association's National Championship Show. The first three in each class will qualify. Categories are for:

Small hack stallion: Exceeding 14.2hh, but not exceeding 15hh. Stallion of hack type suitable to breed a show hack.
Large hack stallion: Exceeding 15hh but not exceeding 15.3hh. Stallion of hack type suitable to breed a show hack.
Small hack broodmare: Certified in foal, or with own foal at foot. Four years old and over, exceeding 14.2hh but not exceeding 15hh.
Foal: Open to progeny from the above category and likely to make a hack at maturity.

> ### • SHOWING YOUNGSTOCK •
>
> *Except for foals, youngstock are shown with manes plaited. Tails should either be pulled or plaited (laced), and foals may have their tails plaited or left natural. Except in the case of foals, heels are trimmed. Led hunters should be shown in either a leather headcollar or bridle. Foals will be shown in just a headcollar. Yearlings may also be shown in a headcollar, but a bridle with plain snaffle bit is more usual. Two- and three-year-old hunters should definitely have bits in, and three-year-olds may wear a double bridle.*

Large hack broodmare: Certified in foal, or with own foal at foot. Four years old and over, exceeding 15hh but not exceeding 15.3hh.
Foal: Open to progeny from the above category, and likely to make a hack at maturity.
Small hack yearling: Filly, colt or gelding to make between 14.2hh and 15hh at maturity. Not exceeding 14.1hh on the day.
Large hack yearling: Filly, colt or gelding to make between 15hh and 15.3hh at maturity. Not exceeding 15hh on the day.
Small hack two-year-old: Two-year-old filly, colt or gelding to make between 14.2hh and 15hh at maturity. Not to exceed 14.2hh on the day.

(Top right) Nothing is more important than food! In-hand hunter classes are for hunter broodmares with foal at foot

(Right) This is one of John and Sue Rawding's hunter foals – note how obedient it is, and how well it stands: this is no fluke, but good training

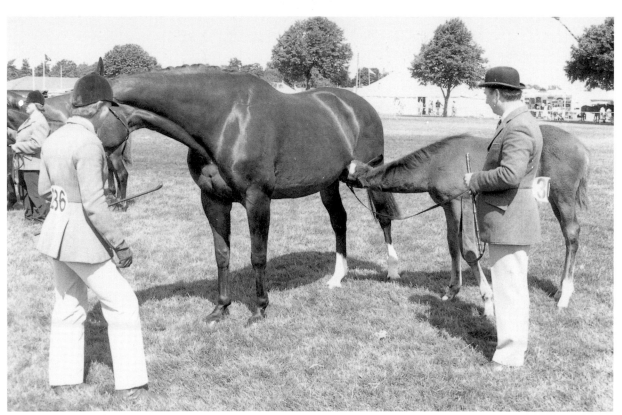

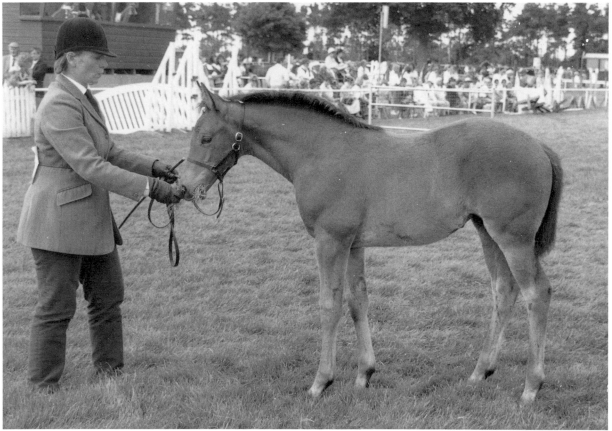

Hunter youngstock. This is Melford Cornish Gold shown by Brian King as a three-year-old (J.E.L. Mayes)

(Top left) Wendy's yearling hunter. Some shows will split classes for fillies and geldings if there are enough entries to warrant it

(Below left) Royal Mile was purchased by Julia Topham Barnes in 1993, and produced by Anne and Allister, becoming Champion In-Hand Hack Breeding at the Three Counties Show

Large hack two-year-old: Two-year-old filly, colt or gelding to make between 15hh and 15.3hh at maturity. Not to exceed 15.1hh on the day.
Small hack three-year-old: Three-year-old filly, colt or gelding to make between 14.2hh and 15hh at maturity. Not to exceed 14.3hh on the day.
Large hack three-year-old: Three-year-old filly, colt or gelding to make between 15hh and 15.3hh at maturity. Not to exceed 15.2hh on the day.

The same presentation guides apply as for in-hand hunter breeding classes. Similar breeding classes are also being introduced for cobs and riding horses, which can only be good for the ridden exhibitor in the future.

ARABS

As with ridden Arabs, classes are for pure-bred, Anglo and part-bred Arabs.

(Above) In-hand Arab classes are as for ridden Arab classes

(Top right) In-hand show ponies are shown in categories for height. This is Cosford Pentangle
(Right) Cosford Pentangle winning the Royal Norfolk Show for the second year running with Oliver Hood

BREEDING SHOW PONIES

These classes run along the same lines as the in-hand hunter stock, but relate to ridden show ponies. For example, there are classes for broodmares and foals, all youngstock and in-hand hunter ponies of the various heights as stipulated in Chapter 5. In order to ensure that ponies will not exceed a certain height at maturity, there is a maximum height allowed on the day for the various classes, and a veterinary surgeon can be called to carry out a measuring at the discretion of the judge if there is any doubt.

NATIVES

Native breeds are shown in their natural state, with flowing manes and tails, although one long plait at the top of the mane is used on some breeds to accentuate the line of the throat and to prevent a thick mane from disguising the head if blown forwards.

The following is a brief guide to the native breeds.

Dales

Height: Not exceeding 14.2hh
Colours: Black, brown, bay, grey and occasionally roan.
Brief description: Short, strong back with good quarters. Variable bone, plentiful silky feathers. Good hard feet. Overall appearance: pony-type cob with keen action, typical pony head.

Highland

Height: Not exceeding 14.2hh
Colours: Grey and dun (mouse, yellow and cream), fox colour with silver mane and tail and black and brown which are not as common today as they used to be.
Brief description: Immensely strong but very docile, with a well carried and attractive head. Broad forehead between bright, kind eyes. Strong, but not overly short neck, with arched crest and flowing mane. Short back with slight natural curve. Deep chest and ribs. An eel-stripe along the back and zebra marks on the forearm are typical, but not always present. Hocks are broad, clean, flat and closely set. Free, and straight action.

Fell

Height: Not exceeding 14hh, no lower height limit.
Colours: Black, brown, bay or grey; preferably no white markings, though a star or a little white on the hind feet is allowed.

Native breeds are shown in their natural state, and there is a range of classes, from mares and foals to best of breed

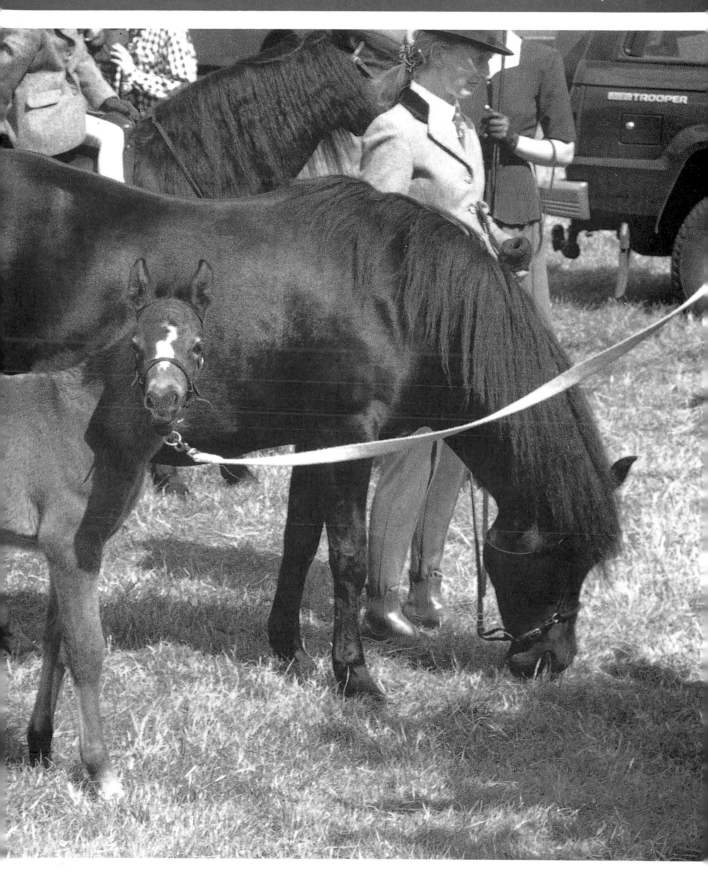

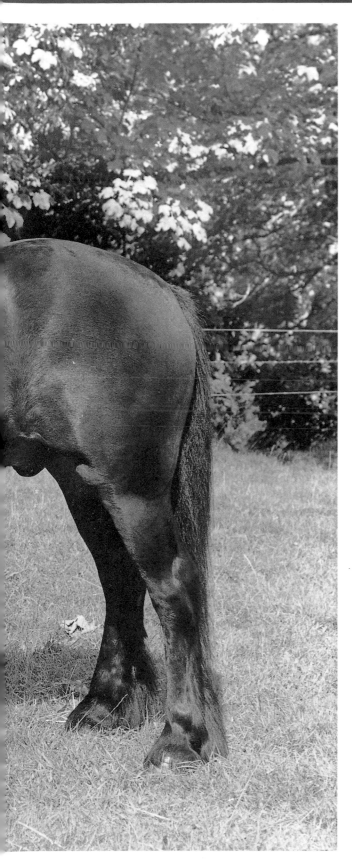

Brief description: Small, well set-on head, chiselled in outline, with a broad forehead tapering to nose. Well laid-back and sloping shoulders, not too fine at the withers. Good thighs and second thigh, well let down and clean cut. Appearance of hardiness peculiar to mountain ponies.

Connemara

Height: 13hh to 14.2hh.
Colours: Predominantly grey, but also black, bay, dun and brown. Some roan and chestnut, but these are fairly rare.
Brief description: Intelligent pony type, with quality head. An easy, low action with a good depth of girth and nice sloping shoulder. Often crossed with Thoroughbreds or Arabs, making nice riding horses or small or lightweight hunters.

New Forest

Height: Maximum 14.2hh, no lower limit.
Colours: Any colour except piebald, skewbald or blue-eyed cream.
Brief description: A good type of riding pony. Short back with strong loins and quarters. Well set-on head with neck a little short from throat to chest, but good laid-back shoulder. Short cannon bones, good feet and tail well set on.

Welsh Mountain, Section A

Height: 12hh maximum.
Colours: Dominant grey, but also roan, chestnut, bay, brown, dun, cream, black and palomino.
Brief description: Hardy, spirited and pony-like, often with Arab characteristics. Small, well set-on, clean-cut head tapering to the muzzle, with bold eyes. Lengthy neck with ample room at angle of the jaw. Long and sloping, well laid-back shoulders. Muscular and well coupled loins and back. Quick, free actions, straight from the shoulder.

Marlingdyke Millstream, twice reserve male champion at the Fell Pony Society breed show, and points winner at the 1993 breed show

• SHOWING WELSH MOUNTAIN PONIES •

While Welsh Mountain ponies should be shown in their natural state, a little discreet trimming may help to improve their appearance. The long hairs under the jaw and those protruding from the ear may be trimmed off, leaving as natural a line as possible; also the whiskers round the muzzle may be shortened. One long thin plait is usually put at the top of the mane behind the ear, the reason being to show off the line of the throat. The tail should look natural, but a tail bandage may help persuade it to lie flat at the top if the hairs are very bushy. This should be removed before entering the ring (The Welsh Pony and Cob Society).

Welsh ponies, Section B

Height: Up to 13.2hh.
Colours: As for Section A.
Brief description: A riding pony with quality, also free action, and adequate bone and substance. Same attributes as Section A.

Welsh ponies of cob type, Section C

Height: Not exceeding 13.2hh.
Colours: As for Section A.
Brief description: A cross between the Welsh Mountain pony and the Welsh Cob. Strong, hardy and active cob type, with pony character. As much substance as possible is most desirable. A quality head, full of pony character. A modest quantity of silky feathers is not objectionable, but thick coarse ones are.

Welsh Cobs, Section D

Height: No height limit applies.
Colours: Any, except piebald and skewbald.
Brief description: A smart and stylish animal of quality. Powerful loins and quarters, and short coupled. Plenty of substance and stamina. Powerful hocks and good, strong hooves.

(Welsh part-bred horses are becoming very popular, but there are very few showing classes for them and generally these horses are shown in the mainstream of riding horse and hunter classes.)

Exmoor

Height: Mares not exceeding 12.2hh; stallions and geldings not exceeding 12.3hh.
Colours: Bay, brown or dun with black points, mealy markings on muzzle, round the eyes and inside the flanks. No white markings anywhere.
Brief description: Wide forehead, short thick ears. Toad eye. Legs clean and short, with strong cannon bone and hard, well-shaped feet. Definite 'pony character'; hard and strong; vigorous, alert and symmetrical in appearance. Tail is neatly set in, lower than most ponies.

Dartmoor

Height: Not exceeding 12hh.
Colours: Any colours except piebald and skewbald, although bay, black or brown is preferable. Excessive white is discouraged.
Brief description: Small, well set-on, 'blood-like' head. Ears very small and alert. Neck strong, but not too heavy, long or short. Hindquarters, back and loins strong and well muscled. Tough, well shaped feet. Tail is set high and is full. Movement low and free, with no knee action.

• JOHN RAWDING ON SHOWING YOUNGSTOCK •

John Rawding has very definite views on showing youngstock:

'I never show yearlings. Yearlings need time to grow and come to themselves, without all the paraphernalia of showing. You often see yearlings carted about from show to show, and then by the time they are four they are absolutely fed up with the whole job, and if you've got one that has a lot of quality as a yearling, it will have lost that by the time it is four. I only show my two-year-olds half-a-dozen times, for a similar reason. By the time they get to three, however, as long as you have got the right type of horse, I don't think it matters so much if they are shown more. I never show any horse a great deal, in any case. Half-a-dozen times a year is ample, and the rest of the time they are having as natural a life as possible out in the field.'

Shetland

Height: Average of 40in (102cm), registered stock must not exceed 40in (102cm) at three years old, and 42in (107cm) at four years old.

Colours: A foundation colour of black, but any colour except spotted is acceptable.

Brief description: The strongest member of the horse world in relation to its size. A small, but well shaped looking head. Broad forehead with sensible expression. Strong, muscular neck with good crest. Thickset, deep-ribbed body. Short back, broad in chest with strong and muscular loins. Strong and muscular hind legs and thighs. Tough, round and well shaped feet. Straight, full action, both in front and behind, bending the knees and hocks well.

OTHER BREEDS AND CATEGORIES

Donkeys

There has been a great revival in donkey showing in the past few years, with classes well attended. Classes are for mares and foals, youngstock (colts, fillies and geldings), for best pet donkey and for best condition and turnout.

(Above) Champion Shetland Pony at the 1994 Royal Norfolk Show

(Below) There has been a great revival in donkey showing, although this one's not too impressed – 'This showing game's a breeze!'

As well as mature horses, there are also classes for foals and youngstock throughout all the breed categories

Heavy horses

These classes are very popular, and horses are either shown in hand or in harness (known in the heavy-horse world as 'turnout classes'). There are classes for all the heavy breeds; most commonly at the agricultural shows these are for the Suffolk Punch, the Shire, the Percheron and the Clydesdale.

Irish Draught

The Irish Draught is used extensively to cross with the Thoroughbred to produce hunters and competition horses. The horses which result from such a breeding plan are often very successful in mainstream show classes. There are a few shows which hold classes for pure-bred Irish Daughts; in these the horses have both mane and tail plaited, but it is acceptable to have the feathers intact.

Cleveland Bay

There are in-hand classes for both pure and part-bred Cleveland Bays at some shows, although the part-breds are often shown in mainstream hunter classes. Pure-bred Cleveland Bays should be bay, with black points; the only white allowed is a small star on the forehead.

Skewbald and piebald horses

Skewbald and piebald horses are predominantly types rather than breeds, with the notable exception of Icelandics and Shetlands, and increasingly the 'foreign' and 'continental' breeds, where a number of pure-bred coloureds are emerging. Apart from the above, exhibits are expected to conform in overall type characteristics to the categories in which they may be shown, namely: hunter, riding horse, native, lightweight (Thoroughbred/Arab or hack types) cob or hack, for example. The British Skewbald and Piebald Association (BSPA) holds classes for in-hand horses, best colour and markings, and ridden, where horses are expected to give a ridden display if time permits, as with riding horses. There is a strong emphasis on ride, manners and training.

(Top) Classes for heavy horses are always very popular with spectators, and well attended by exhibitors. A Shire's preparation takes considerable dedication

(Above) A pure-bred Irish Draught stallion; Draught stallions are used on Thoroughbred mares to produce hunters and competition horses

(Opposite) Westacre Copelia, an imported riding pony from Britain, has made a tremendous impact on the Australian scene since her arrival; she has won numerous championships in both ridden and led classes. The British pony has made a tremendous impact on the Australian show scene in general (Kate Ames)

Hackney horses

Hackney classes are divided into horses over 14hh and ponies not exceeding 14hh. Hackneys are shown in a four-wheeled vehicle known as a show wagon. The hackney is graceful, quick and elegant; it has a lively personality and loves an audience, which makes it an ideal show horse. Occasionally quick-tempered, it has the brilliance of personality and the glamorous action of a star, and likes nothing better than to perform in front of an admiring group of spectators. Its high prancing action, proud head, and the overall charming spectacle of the elegant horse and driver pulling the attractive show wagon has made it a favourite in the show ring in the UK now for many years.

THE BREEDERS AND EXHIBITORS

In-hand showing for youngstock is the breeder's shop window. A lot of people breed a horse and then find it is fun to show it and educate it along the way. For people who are serious breeders, and stallion owners, the youngstock classes provide an excellent opportunity to show off their stock. People are always interested in the breeding of horses, so if your mare breeds a foal that does well, it gives her stock more value and also that of the stallion.

In Australia there are probably two types of show competitor representing two different industries: first, the breeding industry which focuses on breed/halter classes, and accordingly most of these competitors would be breeders who run a stud. Second, the hacking community, where most competitors would have other jobs, hacking for a hobby rather than a living, and preparing horses from their homes.

Even so, in the Arabian, Western and hacking communities there are professional trainers who undoubtedly dominate things to a certain extent. Large studs, for example, have trainers to prepare their horses for 'halter' classes, particularly in the Arabian world. In the hacking community, Vicki and Chris Lawrie are professional producers, in that they take in other people's horses to train and show professionally – which they do very successfully: they currently have a galloway, Pure Castle, who has been all but undefeated for the last two years. Others, such as the Walker family, train and show

• AUSTRALIA'S TOPS •

Maureen, Bruce and Lindy Walker are the principals of Marena Stud and Riding Academy, and are one of Australia's most prominent breeders of Australian stud book ponies, Australian stock horses, and riding ponies. Since Marena's establishment in 1974 it has won a total of 151 Royal Show championships at Sydney, Melbourne, Perth, Launceston, Hobart, Adelaide and Canberra. It has also won 40 NSW (New South Wales) state titles and 21 national titles.

'It is the stud's ambition to win champion in all three hack categories at one Royal,' says Maureen. 'Several times we have won two of them, for example Champion Hack with Marena Viva and Champion Pony Hack with Marena Mayflower at Brisbane Royal in 1983.'

Maureen considers the Sydney Royal Easter Show to be the major show in Australia: 'It is the biggest, and has the most competitors from other states. Melbourne Royal would run a close second,' she says.

Lindy Walker has consistently won riding classes and championships throughout her showing career. Her first Royal Show Champion Rider title was won at Brisbane Royal in 1974 when she was ten years old, in the class for children under seventeen years. She is believed to be the youngest rider ever to achieve this position. By the end of 1994, her totals at Melbourne, Sydney, Brisbane, Adelaide, and Perth Royals were twenty-six Royal Show rider championships, and thirty-one Royal Show horse champions!

'All my major wins are special to me, but if I had to really choose there would still be two ultimates,' she says. 'Winning the Garryowen, and winning five Royal Show riding championships in a row! I would also still like to win Champion Hack at Sydney Royal.'

In the Garryowen's fifty-eight year history, it has only been won by seven NSW riders, and Lindy is the only NSW competitor to have won the trophy since 1972. An impressive record.

their own horses full time. On the whole, however, whether in the UK, Australia or the USA, most showing competitors have only one or perhaps two horses, so showing is purely a hobby; the few others have a string of animals which occupy them full time, so they follow the circuits and therefore appear to dominate the industry.

THE USA IN-HAND SCENE

Horses are shown in-hand in what are known as breeding, halter, in-hand, model or Bella Forma classes. In all breeds, horses are shown in-hand – or led – by handlers to be judged on their conformation, substance, quality and adherence to breed standards. Those with transmittable unsoundnesses are heavily penalized. Horses are usually entered in classes by breed, so that qualifications of the breed are judged against their own standard. Classes are divided by the age and sex of the horses. Animals are often walked and trotted in front of the judges to be evaluated on their way of moving and their potential to perform.

The most popular breed classes are for the

Horse and handler competing in a USA Stock Horse Halter Class

following: the Arabian; Connemara; Hackney; Morgan; national show horse (a mix of Arabian and American Saddlebred); Paso Fino; American Saddlebred; Quarter Horse; Mustang; Appaloosa; Shetland pony and Welsh pony and Welsh Cob. Breed associations generally have their own set of rules for showmanship, but at certain shows classes may be governed by the AHSA.

THE SHOW MARE AT STUD

A broodmare's time for showing in the summer is limited because of her breeding activity. Ideally a showing broodmare should have an early foal so that she can return to stud early in the year, and be confirmed back in foal before you want to start showing her; then she need not miss out important classes due to the fact that she is foaling! However, it is not advisable to cart young foals about too much; the travelling and bustle of show days can be extremely tiring on their young legs and joints, so it is essential that they are not over-shown. A good breeder will select the most appropriate shows carefully, with thought given to the foal's welfare, and the mare's chance to do well.

A mare that is in foal early in the year need not miss out on important classes; however, caution must be practised in order not to over-show young foals

DRESS FOR IN-HAND CLASSES

When leading horses in mainstream showing classes in the UK, men should wear a suit, or a coat and trousers; collar and tie; and a bowler hat. Women may wear a coat and trousers, with a collar and tie, or must otherwise be tidily and neatly dressed. Flapping dresses and large-rimmed hats are definitely not a good idea – yet you do see women showing in such dress; however, it is unprofessional and far from safe, so if you want to create a good impression, wear something more suitable! Similarly, dangling earrings or long necklaces are not a good idea. Remember, you will have to run in order to trot your horse out, so ensure you have on boots or shoes that will not slip or rub. In native classes you often see handlers wearing trainers so they can run very fast alongside their speedy ponies, and as long as the trainers are conservative there is nothing wrong in this. It is a good idea to wear gloves, to prevent your hands from getting sore if your youngster becomes excitable and constantly pulls.

In Australia, Arabian handlers dress up almost in 'evening wear', particularly for classic and evening shows, where they will wear 'black tie' turnout. With Quarter Horses and Western-type Arabian classes, handlers wear Western gear, with trousers, boots, hat and gloves. In led 'hack' and 'galloway' classes, which are becoming more common, handlers may wear their riding clothes, that is, jodhpurs, riding coat and short boots.

GOOD MANNERS

Horses, whether youngsters or not, must have manners and respect for their handlers. They should be expected to stand and to trot up without constantly fidgeting, nipping or whinnying. In general they must do as they are told, and while you can forgive the occasional wild display, constant misbehaviour should not be tolerated. But while youngsters can become a little wild, and also wobbly in response to the showing atmosphere, they should have had the correct training at home so they know what is expected of them, and will behave to this acceptable level most of the time.

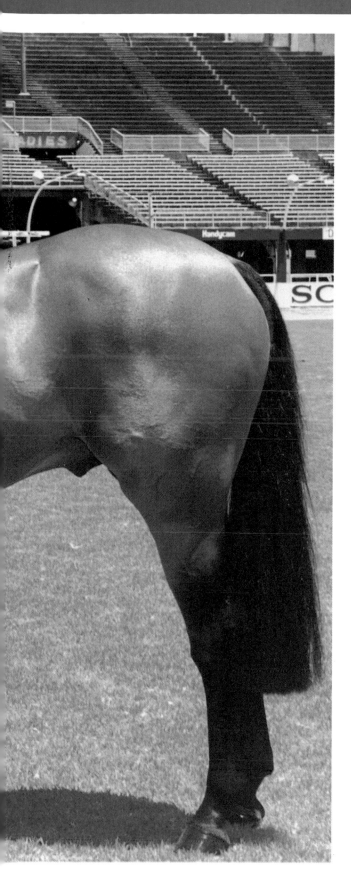

Professional showmen appreciate that horses are not machines and that many need to 'let off steam' on occasion – if you constantly scold your horse for every little thing he does out of order, you are in danger of turning him sour, or into a time-bomb ready to explode, and when he does so it will be when you least expect it. Horses that win are those that want to 'show' themselves. In other words, they are born 'show-offs', and unfortunately this is not something you can create, they either have it, or they do not.

• NO-NONSENSE HANDLING •

It is well known in the UK that John Rawding's horses always behave themselves in the ring. Why?

'It has a lot to do with the fact that John has always been used to handling stallions,' says Sue. 'As handling stallions is a no-nonsense job, he just gives off an air of commanding respect, and our horses do respect him, right from square one.'

'People think I lead my horses a lot,' says John, 'when in fact I don't lead them from one show to the next. However, they have had manners instilled into them from the beginning, and they know they have to behave. If you teach a horse to respect you from the outset, it knows the "rules", and as such you can always treat the horse fairly. If it is punished for misbehaving it will know why, and similarly if it is rewarded.

'About two years ago I took a two-year-old to the Royal and we had only put a bit in its mouth five days before it went. It then had a crash course in leading and went on to win the filly class. The horse respected me and I respected the horse, so all's fair. After all, the only reason you show horses is for pleasure – well, it certainly isn't for the money, is it?'

Super Supreme Led Exhibit at the NSW Riding Pony Show. Silkwood Chalk Stream (stallion), owned by Tony Oliver Watkins and Margaret Giles of Sydney (Trich Matthews)

10

JUDGING

JUDGES: THE QUALITIES REQUIRED

Who *are* judges? Generally, they are people who have been about horses a long time and who have had a great deal of experience. They also have to go through a considerable probation period, judging under a more experienced judge before they are accepted onto the society panels; in this way the societies can be sure that the people they ask to judge really do know what they are doing.

> ### • MALE JUDGES •
> *'What I would like to see,' says John Rawding, 'although I don't know how we are going to achieve it, is more male judges. I don't want to appear disrespectful to ladies, but a small lady judge has got to be a brilliant jockey to be able to ride big, strong, middle- and heavyweight horses. I would love to see many more young men coming into the job, but unfortunately it is a sign of the times that they just cannot afford to do it.'*

What makes a good or a bad judge?

Those who have a background of experience with horses, such as buying and selling, or having plenty of horses passing through their hands, are likely to be good judges of horses. In years gone by there were plenty of such 'nagsmen', but sadly they are a dying breed. The variety of horses one has come into contact with is important in this respect. A judge needs to be able to spot the right type of horse for the class, but he also needs to be able to sort the wheat from the chaff. While a professional showperson may have had a great many good horses pass through his hands, it doesn't necessarily make him a good judge of horses as he needs to have had experience of bad horses too, so he can make comparisons between types of horse. Perhaps it is not with much conscious thought, but

a keen horseman will always evaluate a horse at first glance. Thus a judge has to know good conformation, and needs to be able to assess fully the horse's ability and ride in the minute or two that he is able to ride it.

There is sometimes a considerable difference in the riding standard of judges. For the best judges, all the horses in the class go well; for the worst

Generally judges are people who have had a lot of experience with a great variety of horses. The judges of the 1994 Cob of the Year championships at Wembley: Mr C. Castle and Mrs S.M. Nelson

judges, horses are often seen to go badly, even resentfully. There are two types of judge who sooner or later become known for what they are. The first is the judge with bad hands, who does not get on well with horses with sensitive mouths, but loves the horse which takes a hold. He will soon acquire a reputation of being 'mutton-fisted', and will find fewer well schooled, sensitive horses

For the best judges, all the horses in the class go well; for the worst, you can often see horses going badly

before him, as competitors value their horses' mouths. The other type of judge is the 'form' judge, who bases his decisions on how well the horse has done at previous shows – in short, a judge who judges faces and not horse-flesh. This type of judge is simply playing safe because he lacks the courage of his own convictions or simply prefers not to 'rock the boat'.

'A good judge is a fair judge who judges on manners, conformation and ride, not on the rider's or handler's face,' says Wendy. 'The judge's job is a very difficult one, as he or she can never please everyone. In fact, he will probably only please one or two people in every class, and they will be the people at the top of the line.'

'There are judges and judges,' says Allister. 'Basically what we do is vote with our feet. If we don't think the judge is going to suit our horses, or we know for a fact that they are going to put so-and-so up, then we don't go to that particular show.'

According to John Rawding, what makes a good judge is akin to the old adage, 'How long is a piece of string?' And according to Sue Rawding, a good

• AN EYE FOR A HORSE •

According to Vin Toulson, good judges are sadly very few and far between: 'The two essentials are wide experience and a natural "eye for a horse", and too many of today's judges lack that essential practical experience. Also, an eye for a horse is a gift which comes naturally, or not at all. Further essentials which are too often lacking are integrity and self-confidence; for example, too many horses and ponies win because their owners or riders will be judging a horse belonging to the judge at a future show, or because the judge knows that the horse has won at recent shows; or perhaps he or she is not self-confident enough not to be influenced by the fact that a competitor has extensively sponsored the prize money at the show.'

A good judge is one that judges manners, conformation and ride alone, and not the handler's, or rider's face

judge is preferably one who has learnt by his mistakes through his pocket. 'Your best judges, without any shadow of a doubt, are your professional riders and producers,' says John Rawding. As a rider and judge herself, Sue agrees with this. 'All professional riders will know that they often win classes they shouldn't have, and lose classes they should have won. When you are stood in line you will know how your horse has gone for you, and how it has carried the judge, and so you should know basically where you should be placed on the day. Whether you actually end up in the right place is another matter, but because professionals are in this situation day in, day out, they do make the best judges, as they are not going to go into any ring and make a fool of themselves.'

'It's really quite simple,' says John. 'In the UK there are shows nearly every day of the week, and if you don't respect who is judging at a particular show you don't go, and that is the end of the story.'

If being a judge is such a hard task, why does anyone do it? Well, it certainly is not for the money, as usually only expenses are paid. The real reason is that there is considerable prestige attached to being asked to judge at a leading show; this is what all 'apprentice' judges hope to achieve.

THE CODE OF CONDUCT FOR JUDGES

What is the judge's job in the ring?

The judge's job is to judge each horse on the day: he is there to give each horse a fair assessment. If a particular judge is a little strong in his style, well so be it – at least each horse gets the same treatment. If the horse is going to go well on the day, then it goes well, but if it decides to be silly and tense then it is not going to go, it is as simple as that. At the end of the day each horse gets the same ride, and it is up to the horse to behave and give a good ride; it is not up to the judge to 'school' the horse in the ring.

There are certain unspecified 'rules' which govern a judge's suitability for the job, a sort of code of conduct; these include the following:

A judge should:
• know the specifications for each individual class

• THE JUDGE'S JOB •

According to Sue Rawding, the judge's job in the ring is to watch everything that is humanly possible, without being distracted by other things happening at the ringside, or chatty stewards. 'Perhaps all anyone can ask of a judge is that he truly does his best, to the best of his ability. No judge can do more than that.'

• know what constitutes both good and bad conformation for a certain type or breed of horse
• know what constitutes correct action and performance for a certain type or breed of horse
• use uniform criteria when judging so that each horse is judged as fairly as the next
• be efficient and pleasant, so that each class appeals to spectators as well as competitors
• be responsible for his own actions and opinions, even when judging within a panel of judges
• not fraternize with competitors, except in a public area where all competitors are welcome
• discharge from the ring any unruly horse that

The judge's job is not always an easy one. Some horses are difficult, and some shouldn't even be in the ring. Wendy in the throes of judging a rather difficult customer in the heavyweight cob class

presents a danger to others in the ring
• not discuss the sale or purchase of horses while in an official capacity
• dismiss an unsound horse from the ring, or take advice from the show's veterinary surgeon, if one is present
• have no financial commitment or interest in any horse entered, as this casts doubt on impartiality
• have no business relationship with any competitor, as this casts doubt on impartiality
• aim to be constructive and helpful to exhibitors where possible.

What is the judge looking for?

Allister has very definite and considered views as to what a judge is looking for; he is himself a judge for the British Show Hack, Cob and Riding Horse Association and is therefore well qualified to comment.

(Left) Wendy takes a good look during the initial walk round, as this is when an initial line-up is being formed in the judge's mind

(Below) When judging, Wendy always aims to be constructive and helpful to exhibitors when possible

initial pull-in. Then of course the horses have their gallop and another of your initial line-up might start to buck, and so you are down to one –although this one is far from being the winner at this stage. However, this process does allow you to bring them into line in a rough order of preference.

'While an initial impression is very important, a good judge also needs to be able to see through this. Take a local show, for example, where you get a huge variety of horses and riders within the same class. Maybe one horse appears in front of you wearing a big fluffy numnah and a bridle that is not correctly fitted, with a rider that is not particularly well turned out – in short, the whole turnout looks hideous. Next to this is a nice, but fairly ordinary little horse that is beautifully presented, and it is going really nicely. The well presented horse is pulled in first, and your fluffy numnah horse ends up way down the line. However, when you ride the well presented horse you find it is not really as nice as you initially thought. Then you take a good look at the fluffy numnah horse, and although its whole presentation is wrong, when you get on, it gives you a fantastic ride; and when the saddle is removed you find that, piece for piece, its conformation is really good – so "fluffy numnah" then moves up.

'The initial impression is all-important. If when a horse enters the ring everything looks "right", then the judge will look again at that horse. You can often pick out the first three or four horses in the line-up, just by looking at them during the initial walk round; the horses that grab your attention at this point are certainly going to get that second look. However, when they all move into trot you might have to alter your opinion, because one of your initial selection might become really fizzy, while another might move like a camel – so horses are being chosen gradually by a process of elimination, and from your initial view of four very nice horses you might be left with only two for the

• THE JUDGES'S OPINION •

G.W. Evans, general secretary and chief executive of the National Light Horse Breeding Society comments: 'I am aware that judges' opinions do vary, but they should not vary too much when it comes to the assessment of conformation and action, as it is either right or wrong. In ridden classes the ride is all-important, of course, and only the judge knows what sort of ride a horse is giving him.

'As far as judging faces is concerned, in the vast majority of cases this is a fallacy. The point is that the professionals are experts at obtaining and producing top class horses; these are well schooled and always give the judge a good ride. However, there are now classes for amateurs at quite a number of shows and these classes are very popular; they have a championship at the Royal International Horse Show, with qualifying classes throughout the country beforehand.'

As John Rawding knows, the show's not over until the 'steward drops his arm', so he does not allow his horse to slacken at the last moment. Such attention to detail can often swing the judge's opinion in your favour if the choice is a difficult one

• THE FINAL DECISION •

'When I am judging,' says Sue Rawding, 'I am always looking for the horse I've missed. When I ride the horses, there is no one more pleased than me to find a horse that I had overlooked on the initial walk round. It gives me great pleasure to move up such a horse, because it is deserved.

'If I come up against two horses of similar quality, the last walk round will often split them. At this point I am being far more critical of every step, and sooner or later one emeres as the winner.' So competitors, take note – the show's not over until the steward drops his arm!

'To the uneducated person this decision will be wrong, and you will hear mutterings around the ringside of "Why on earth has he put that one up?" This is because the bystander cannot see through the fluffy numnah and the shabby rider. However, it *is* a judge's job to do that, and if it makes him unpopular, then so be it. Judging is a very personal thing. It's about weighing up the pros and the cons on the day. There is no such thing as a perfect animal, so you have to decide in your opinion which you prefer. Horses can help you out, as some tend to judge themselves in a small way. Many of even the nicest horses may fall short in some respect along the line at a particular show, yet behave brilliantly at another show and come top.'

Lady Zinnia Judd and David Hunt deliberate over the championship

• A GOOD OR BAD JUDGE •

Anne Sturges says:

'The good judge must "judge on the day" and have the courage of his or her own convictions. This means judging the best horse on the day rather than on form and who is showing it. I also believe that for hunter breeding he or she must have a sound knowledge of *breeding* horses, not just riding them. It takes a great deal of breeding experience to be able to judge, particularly foals. I also think the good judge always has time after classes to give advice to any exhibitors who ask for it. Encouragement is everything.

'The bad judge doesn't have the courage of his or her convictions, turning a blind eye to ill-mannered horses because of the person riding or showing them and, for the same reason, is not able to place the *best* horse in the class. In extreme cases they also cannot tell a lame horse from a sound one!'

Betty Powell has been showing and judging horses and ponies of all types for many decades; she is on the panel of judges for the National Light Horse Breeding Society, the British Show Pony Society, the Ponies Association (UK) and the British Driving Society (BDS), as well as being a member of the BDS judges' committee. She is thus well able to speak on judges' behaviour:

'It has been standard practice all my lifetime that these simple rules are followed: you are not seen talking to competitors before the classes begins; you adopt a friendly, cheerful and very busy attitude when judging; you answer any remarks put to you in the ring by competitors in the shortest possible way; and after the classes are over, you should be quite happy to answer any queries from a competitor outside the ring, but never in the horsebox area.

'When judging, you are representing the society which has selected you for its panel. You have an

Some shows have a system where one judge assesses conformation while another rides the horses. At Wembley the horses are taken outside the arena for the conformation assessment

extremely important task in hand, and this needs total concentration. Believe me, when – mostly in the riding pony world – you are faced with classes of up to forty look-alikes of the same height, three or four classes in succession, plus a championship, you need all your faculties!

'At the start of the day when I don my judge's hat, all thoughts of socializing go out of the window. The fun days are when I'm either competing or "there for the beer".'

THE JUDGE'S DECISION – IS IT FINAL?

The judge's decision is definitely final on the day: once he has given his opinion, that is it. If you feel strongly enough about a particular judge you can put forward your complaints, and if enough people feel the same way the judge can be removed from the judges' panel. However, while this might be a long-term solution to bad judging, it is cold comfort for those who feel cheated on the day because: 'You are never going to alter the result on the day,' says Allister. 'Organisers are not going to say "Oh dear, everyone is upset so we will judge that class again". You might do well one day when you think you shouldn't have done so well, and you accept that as good luck. Similarly you might think you should have done better than you have, and you accept that as bad luck. If you can't accept the judge's decision you shouldn't be in the ring. It is very hard sometimes, but that's showing!

'I do think the system of one judge for conformation and another for ride is good. I know it can sometimes cause a certain amount of controversy, but it does speed the job along which benefits both horses and competitors, and makes it less boring for spectators.'

• QUERYING THE JUDGE'S DECISION •

Vin Toulson says:

'If you want to ask the judge why you have been put down, do it at some later date, not in the ring. And if you cannot take seemingly unjustifiable disappointments, don't go in for showing!'

11

THE ROAD TO WEMBLEY

Wembley is entirely a show on its own. Furthermore the preparation for it is very different to that for agricultural shows. You have to have the horses much more obedient and relaxed and happier in their work before Wembley, because the show has a charged atmosphere; mentally as well as physically they have to be that much more advanced in their preparation. In your run-up to Wembley you must try very hard to have your horse going better than he has ever gone before.

'Having your horse relaxed is the key,' says Allister, 'because you never know how a horse will react to Wembley. In fact, they are often worse the second time they go, not the first, because then they know what to expect – they remember it from the time before.'

• PREPARING THE HORSE FOR WEMBLEY •
Wendy explains how difficult it is to prepare a horse for Wembley:

'The horse's coat is starting to change as the show is in October and the horse is thus preparing for winter. He needs to be very heavily rugged up early on, unless you decide to clip him before the show. Colour is a major factor here. Greys are very easy because they stay the same colour underneath when clipped, but chestnuts and bays often look rather "wishy-washy" because their coat hasn't come through and so they haven't got a lot of colour about them; so preparation for Wembley is very individual for each horse. If your horse gets a really woolly coat then you haven't got much choice but to clip, because he will stand out like a sore thumb.'

QUALIFICATION

Wembley is very difficult to qualify for. There are a great many shows that hold qualifiers up and down the country, but usually you have to win to qualify, unless you come second to a horse that has already qualified; so it is extremely difficult to do. Once you have got your qualifying ticket, you can consider yourself very lucky; for one thing the pressure is off and you can enjoy the rest of the showing season. If not, you will have to chase the last qualifiers in order to try and succeed, and this may mean travelling miles from home if you are that ambitious.

For Wembley, horses have to be as relaxed, both physically and mentally, as possible

(Right) Wembley – straight ahead! Allister and Cosford Royal Visit make their way to the Wembley arena flanked by the horseboxes on one side, the stables on the other and Wembley stadium in front

WEMBLEY:
EVERY SHOWPERSON'S AIM

Stabling and exercise at the event

It is always advisable to stable at Wembley as exercise areas are very restricted. Also, they are only open at certain times of the day, and usually very early in the morning – about six o'clock, so if you don't get there until 7.30am you have no other opportunity to acclimatize the horse. Besides, it is always as well to get in the ring early so the horses have as long as possible to get used to the arenas, the bright lights and the crowds. The atmosphere is usually electric in the main arena during the afternoon and evening performances and this transmits to both horse and rider. Riders are usually susceptible to a bit of excitement and nerves, and this alerts the horse to something out of the ordinary, so you need to keep yourself calm. Warming up in the indoor collecting arena will help settle you down to the atmosphere and sights and sounds; just take the attitude that you have done very well to get as far as the championships, and that anything else is going to be a real bonus. Some horses find it hard to settle at all; says Allister:

'We made a mistake with the grey hack this year at Wembley because we stabled her at the event for too long, and as time went on she got more and more excited and tense. Ideally you would want to go just the evening before the day of your class, so as to get the veterinary inspection sorted out. If we had a free choice then we would bring our horses on the morning of the show and not stable them at all, but there is never enough time to get them through the vet and working in, so basically you are obliged to go the night before. In our opinion the longer any horse is at Wembley the worse it gets. You have to bear in mind that Wembley is in the heart of London and very few horses are used to such an environment. When you bring a horse to the event it is so different from what he is used to that you are in danger of blowing his mind. Not many horses would be used to such an environment, and by the second night of being

Trotting up during the preliminary judging is always a tense time: everyone wants to make it through to the final judging, but not all can

stabled at Wembley they have usually had enough – they are beginning to think "where's my field".

What to wear

For the preliminary judging at Wembley the same clothes are usually worn as for general showing. Then for the final judging in the evening or afternoon performances, ladies usually wear a navy coat, top hat and stock, and men wear either a black tail-coat or black hunting coat and a velvet cap, or they may wear a red tail-coat and top hat.

What to expect

No amount of describing it will prepare you for your first Wembley. There are so many details you need to know: you can only work in at certain times; you have to collect your number from a certain place; you have to produce a veterinary slip to get your number, and so on; and your horse is bound to be more excitable than usual, too. Seek advice from someone who has been before. Anne describes procedure on arrival:

'The problem is, nothing is made clear to you. If you didn't know about the need to have your veterinary certificate in order to collect your number you could walk half a mile across the showground to get it, only to have to walk back again to collect your vet's certificate, and then back again to collect your number.

'On arrival at the show you are directed onto a parking area and asked to unload your horse. All its rugs are removed and a vet checks its identity and looks through its vaccinations – check these the minute you have qualified, because if the vaccinations are out by even one day, even if this were when the horse was a yearling, you will not be allowed in. And if you forget the certificate you will not be allowed in. The vets will also have a quick glance over the horse, but this is not a thorough examination and you can then load him back up. The next step is to go to the stable manager's office where you are allocated your stable and told where it is; if you do not have a stable booked your horse will stay on its box in the lorry park for the duration of the show.

'You should also find out when you can collect your exhibitor's pass which gets you into the

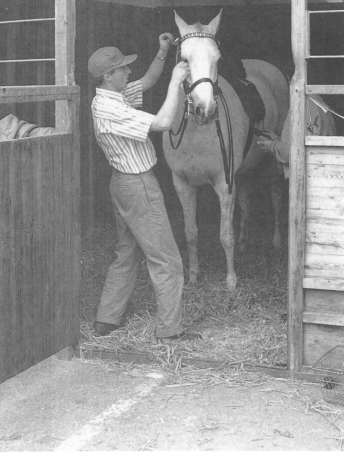

(Above) In the main arena during the afternoon and evening performances, the atmosphere is usually electric. Allister (centre) uses all his showmanship to keep Hamlet calm in the hubbub of activity

(Top left) Tom Cobbley is trimmed within an inch of his life!

(Left) Allister leaves everyone to get on with the preparation of the horse while he goes and finds a quiet spot

complex. The unfortunate thing about this is that you don't get your exhibitor's pass until the day you are showing, so if you arrive on the Tuesday in readiness for your Wednesday class, you are given a piece of paper allowing you into the stable area only – and that is as far as you get: you can't actually go into the stadium. You can ride into the working areas, but you can't enter them on foot as you haven't got a pass. This means you can't walk up to the riding area to see what time you are allowed to exercise, and it can all become very frustrating. It is certainly tricky for the first-timer.'

Coping with nerves

'You don't get time to be nervous at Wembley!' jokes Allister. 'Obviously, though, you want to do well so you are going to be a little bit more nervous than usual.' Allister copes with his nerves by working his horse, then giving it to Anne to get ready because he prefers to be on his own and doesn't like a lot of people fussing around him. 'The best thing to do,' he says, 'is to sit and have a bottle of sherry with the owners, because the owners are much more nervous than I am, really!'

Doing your best

While it is true for all shows, at Wembley in
particular you cannot do any more than your best.
At Wembley you will have to work your horse so
that it is more relaxed than you would normally
have it before going into the ring. Beware not to do
too much though; this is where being professional
about it counts. Ideally the horse should be
switched off enough, so that when he gets into the
arena there is still just enough excitement to switch
him back on, but without him going over the top.

*Taking the horse into the practice arena early in the day
allows him to become used to all the sights and sounds
that he may never have experienced if he has not been to
a large indoor show before*

*(Right) The practice arena at Wembley: the horse needs to
be relaxed to a point where the atmosphere is just enough
to switch him back on, but not make him boil over*

In the arena

In the main arena there are a great many things to
cope with, such as a huge audience towering above
you in close proximity; bright lights, a cheering
crowd, and so on. You can never prepare your
horse for this, so at the end of the day you have just
got to trust to luck.

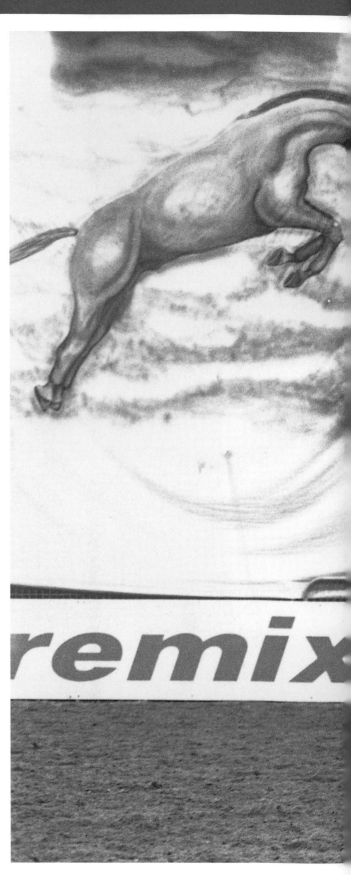

The thrill of winning or being placed

To win at Wembley is the ultimate achievement. There is nothing to beat being pulled in first – it is the culmination of a whole year's work. Even being placed is special. Says Allister:

'You always want to win, but the disappointments are not what they might be if your horse were to stand last at a county show. You have still made the final at Wembley. However, once you have got that far, you are hooked: you acquire a driving ambition to win, and nothing will do but winning which is why you try every year. Obviously there can only be one winner for each class, but you can imagine the thrill of winning a competition that started out as qualifying events around the country with literally hundreds of horses, with riders all hoping to be the best. To win at Wembley is to be the absolute best. The biggest thrill is going down the centre of the ring the spotlight on you if you win – but even being placed at Wembley is a great achievement. To put it all in perspective, you have to remember that even if you only just get into the final judging and come home with a ninth rosette, it should be considered an extreme honour and you have done very well. It means you are ninth in the *country!*

'Wembley is a good social time for owners as well. Because we produce horses for other people we have to try and keep our owners and riders as

relaxed as possible too, so we cannot just think of ourselves. You just have to try and have everything running as soon as possible so they don't get upset.'

MAJOR AUSTRALIAN EVENTS

The Horse of the Year Shows (both EFA and Hack Council) and the Royal Shows are the major events on the Australian showing calendar. Within the Royal Shows there are particular trophies which are coveted by competitors, each for a different reason. It could be said that there is no one show, such as Wembley in the UK, which brings the show world together. The Garryowen Equestrienne Turnout Trophy at Melbourne Royal Show is Australia's second most prominent equine event – the first being the Melbourne Cup Thoroughbred race. Winning Champion Rider at Sydney Royal may be the aspiration of one competitor, and maybe the Crane Trophy for Galloways at Sydney is the ultimate aim of another. Many trophies and cups have historical and prestigious value, and different competitors place different emphasis on different goals. The Australian media would probably place the most importance on the winners at the National

• **THE PRICE OF WINNING** •
'There is nothing that equals the thrill of winning at Wembley,' say John and Sue Rawding. 'However, we do feel that the prize money is ridiculous. At this moment in time, show horses are carrying Wembley, and yet the prize money is abysmal. Even if you were lucky enough to win, your costs in diesel and entry fees to get there, far exceed the cash prize. Winning at Wembley is the goal, but it is definitely not because of what you win, it is why you win: winning at Wembley means that you have the best horse in the country, and that you have produced and shown it better than any other exhibitor there – that's the thrill of Wembley!'

(Above) The biggest thrill is going down the centre of the ring with the spotlight on you. Carol Cooper riding Mystic Minstrel, winning the Small Hack of the Year title at the Horse of the Year Show (Anthony Reynolds)

(Left) Wembley is always spectacular – there simply is not another show like it!

Horse of the Year Show (EFA) and the Grand National Horse of the Year Show (NSW Hack Council). If the same horses and riders win at both, then they deserve to be hailed as champions. Often, however, this is not the case.

Australian showing lifestyles

The Australian hacking scene has many wonderful riders and show horse presenters who would equate to the UK professionals attending Wembley and the Royal International. These personalities consistently produce beautiful, well mannered and spectacularly turned out horses and ponies year after year. Every season sees the emergence of

Some of the sights of Wembley are quite unique – there is no other show like it

her wins in the Pope Cup and Champion Hack. Special wins were Champion Hack on Whitsun at Melbourne Royal and her Garryowen win on Ark Royal in 1992. Caroline comments:

'The ultimate showing event in Australia for me is the Garryowen Trophy at Royal Melbourne Show. It is a special event for a number of reasons. The event is a tribute to the memory of a great horsewoman named Violet Murrell and her champion horse Garryowen; both Violet Murrell and her husband died trying to save Garryowen in a stable fire in 1934. Since that year the Garryowen has been the most coveted trophy to win in Australia. The event itself is judged on a points system:

1 Manners and paces (40) and conformation and soundness (50) – 90
2 Riding – 50
3 General Appearance – 20
4 Saddlery – 20
5 Costume – 20
Total – 200

To win, you must do well in every section, and very well in both your riding and your horse's marks. Both you and your horse must be immaculately turned out, and you must have a good working partnership together. There is a set workout which is quite testing; generally this includes extended trot work, sitting trot, changes of leg at the canter, and a good gallop. The field which competes for the trophy is often up to fifty competitors, and these competitors have also had to qualify at the county agricultural shows first, with wins and champions in the open ridden hack sections. So it is the best of the best competing against one another. It is an enormous thrill to win the event – it would be the most prestigious event for ladies in Australia. I am lucky enough to have won it twice and been placed several times.'

another young star, and perhaps that is one of the wonderful things about the showing industry: there is room for both the young and the experienced, and both learn from one another.

Caroline Wagner is one of the stars of the Australian showing scene. With her beautiful grey gelding Ark Royal she has swept all aside, and her previous very special hack in the same league was Whitsun. Caroline runs a turnout saddlery and equestrian tailoring business along with her husband Peter, and is actively involved in the show horse industry at many levels. Caroline's achievements have been varied and numerous: her best she rates as being the Diamond Jubilee Garryowen 1994, and the 1994 Sydney Royal with

• ROSETTE / RIBBON COLOURS •			
Placing	*UK*	*Australia*	*USA*
1st	red	blue	blue
2nd	blue	red	red
3rd	yellow	white	yellow

12

THE END OF THE SHOW SEASON

After Wembley, or at the end of the show season, most horses deserve a rest. Many will have had a long season, during which they have received constant attention, and so they need time to wind down, both physically and mentally – they need to feel that they have their own space. If a horse has been to Wembley he will have been wearing several rugs, and these need to be removed gradually. Only when you are sure you have hardened him off sufficiently well and he is in the stable with no rugs on can he go out, but you will still have to pick the right time, perhaps waiting until you get a nice sunny autumn day. Turning horses away also gives their feet a chance to recover from the rigours of shoeing. Once the shoes are taken off the nail holes can grow down and any little cracks will grow out.

Allister describes the routine followed in his yard:

'Our horses have their rugs taken off one at a time after Wembley in readiness for turning away. Their feeds are then cut down gradually from four to two a

Once the horse has built up enough coat and the weather is suitable it can be turned away. Snowline, having been roughed off at the end of the 1994 season

At the end of the show season the horse's rugs will need to be removed gradually

day, and then these two will be reduced. They will have their shoes taken off and their feet tidied up by the farrier, and then they will be wormed. Before turning them away you have got to give them time to build up the greases in their coat that you have been brushing out all summer. Once they have grown enough coat, or the weather is suitable, they are turned out. All the horses are still fed twice a day and some will continue to come in at nights. Then just after Christmas the whole showing year begins again!'

Some horses don't have a holiday as they may hunt, or do a few indoor activities through the winter. Providing they are being turned out and are kept sweet, the show season should not be that taxing for any horse. We had a little horse a few years ago which hunted all through each winter and

(Left) Just after Christmas the whole showing year begins again. Anne starts with the paperwork – sending off the entries, making sure vaccinations are up to date: and off we go again…

(Below left) Decisions – Wendy decided this horse was never going to make a top show horse and so she sold him on. He is now an excellent hunter and working hunter. Whether they make it to the top or not, showing is a good education for any youngster

(Right) At the end of the day, showing is a sport from which all can derive benefit. Louenna Hood on True Mint, with father Allister on Face the Music having fun, while also winning the Adult and Child Competition at the Ponies UK Summer Championships. This was the first time this class had been held, but it is likely to become popular in the future

(Below right) Is this youngster what you are looking for – can you tell? That's the game of showing!

was shown each summer without a break, and he thrived – but then his summer was never that taxing for him. It is therefore quite feasible to keep a horse going continually as long as he has a varied life and is kept happy.'

DECISION TIME

The end of the show season is a time to sit down and think about how you have done, and what your aims are for the future. You may not have done particularly well by professional standards, but you may have had a lot of fun. If you really enjoy the horse you have, and derive enormous pleasure from showing him whatever the outcome, then really there is no decision to make.

Professional producers and those with ambitions to make the top do have to sit down and consider their options. For them, it is a question of deciding whether the horse is really suitable. He may not have done that well in the current year, but if he is a youngster he may come out a different horse after a break, so all options need to be considered carefully. Sometimes it becomes clear that certain horses will never make the grade as a show horse, and it is important to sell these on into a more suitable field, perhaps as an eventer or showjumper if they show promise, where they will be happier in themselves. This happened with a horse Wendy called Vital Decision. Wendy always considered

the horse to be much too clever for the game of showing: 'He was far too intelligent and quick-minded, so I suggested to his owners that he be tried as an eventer.' The horse went to Ruth McMullen's yard and, partnered by Terry Boon, went on to achieve great things individually and for the British Young Rider's event team. This was a clear case of finding the right key to unlock the door to a horse's future.

'It is important to sit down and look at how you have done in a season, and then decide whether the horse is worth continuing with,' says Allister. 'If you have done everything you possibly can for a horse and still he hasn't done any good, then he simply isn't good enough for the job, so there is no point in continuing down that road. Young horses can alter, of course, and you will have planned for that, so in this case things may be a bit different.'

For Wendy the end of the show season is also a time to make decisions:

'You would know before Wembley whether your horse was good enough or not, and at this stage you have to decide whether he just didn't suit you, or if he wasn't up to the job, as this will indicate what sort of new owner might suit him. Finding a replacement might not be easy, though. Most show people are always looking out for young, nice types of horse. Even if you are not really in the market for one you are always looking, because it becomes part of your nature if you are a real show person. Usually something comes along which takes your eye, and you decide to start again ready for the next show season. It doesn't matter how many horses you produce, as it is always fun to bring out a young horse – you never know quite what it is going to do! Horses can also improve from season to season – a young horse may grow and mature and make a better horse the following year. Some horses will benefit from a bit of hunting because it

gives them something else to think about. If you are intending to try again with your horse the following season you might decide to give him only a short break after the show season, perhaps a couple or three weeks, and then go hunting up until Christmas for a bit of fun. However, it is very difficult to keep a horse in show condition if you also want to hunt all winter, so you will have to compromise.'

Having made your decisions, it is time to start all over again. As I said in the introduction of this book, showing is a sport dictated by seasons. No two seasons are the same, and no two horses are the same, but that's what makes showing a sport of the unknown, coupled with the judges' opinion of course! I will leave you with a few words, which to me – having seen all that goes on behind the scenes, and all that occurs in the ring – sum up the *sport* of showing:

If you think you are beaten, you are;
If you think you dare not, you don't;
If you'd like to win, but think you can't
It's almost a cinch you won't.

If you think you'll lose, you're lost;
For out in the ring we find
Success begins with a competitor's 'Will' –
It's all in the state of mind.

If you think you're outclassed, you are;
You've got to think high to rise.
You've just got to be sure of yourself
Before you can win the prize

Life's battles don't always go
To the stronger or faster man,
But sooner or later the man who wins
Is the one who thinks he can!

THE ASSOCIATIONS

UK

National Light Horse
  Breeding Soc (HIS)
96 High Street
Edenbridge
Kent TN8 5AR

The British Show Hack,
  Cob and Riding Horse
  Assoc
Chamberlain House
Chamberlain Walk
88 High Street
Coleshill
Nr Birmingham B46 3BZ

The British Show Pony
  Soc
124 Green End Road
Sawtry
Huntingdon
Cambridgeshire PE17 5AX

Ponies Assoc (UK)
Chesham House
56 Green End Road
Sawtry
Huntingdon
Cambridgeshire PE17 5UY

Joint Council of Heavy
  Horse Breed Societies
34 Heather Avenue
Frampton Cotterell
Bristol
Avon BS17 2JR

The Joint Measurement
  Board
British Equestrian Centre
Kenilworth
Warwickshire CV8 2LR

The Arab Horse Soc
Windsor House
Ramsbury
Nr Marlborough
Wiltshire SN8 2PE

The Side Saddle Assoc
Highbury House
19 High Street
Welford
Northampton NN6 6HT

The Cleveland Bay
  Horse Soc
York Livestock Centre
Murton
York YO1 3UF

The Clydesdale Horse Soc
  of Great Britain and
  Ireland
24 Beresford Terrace
Ayr
Ayrshire KA7 2EG

The American Saddlebred
  Assoc of GB
Uplands
Alfriston
East Sussex BN26 5XE

British Palomino Soc
Penrhiwllan
Llandysul
Dyfed SA44 5NZ

British American Quarter
  Horse Soc
38 Orchards Way
Westend
Southampton
Hants SO3 3FB

Western Horseman's Assoc
  of GB
13 East View
Barnet
Herts EN5 5TL

Anglo and Part-Bred Arab
  Owners Assoc
Gosford Farm
Ottery St Mary
Devon EX11 1LX

British Percheron Horse
  Soc
Lodge Farm
Beccles
Suffolk NR34 8HG

British Quarter Horse
  Assoc
4th Street NAC
Stoneleigh Park
Kenilworth
Warwickshire CV8 2LG

British Skewbald and
  Piebald Assoc
West Fen House
High Road
Little Downham
Ely
Cambridgeshire CB6 2TB

Dales Pony Soc
196 Springvale Road
Walkley
Sheffield
S. Yorkshire S6 3NU

Dartmoor Pony Soc
Puddaven Farm
North Bovey
Newton Abbot
Devon TQ13 8RJ

Donkey Breed Soc
Manor Cottage
South Thoresby
Nr Alford
Lincolnshire LN13 0AS

English Connemara Pony
  Soc
2 The Leys
Salford
Chipping Norton
Oxon OX7 5FD

Exmoor Pony Soc
Glen Fern
Waddicombe

Dulverton
Somerset TA22 9RY

The Fell Pony Soc
Riccarton Mill
Newcastleton
Roxburghshire TD9 0SN

Hackney Horse Soc of GB
Clump Cottage
Chitterne
Warminster
Wiltshire BA12 0LL

Irish Draught Horse Soc
  (GB)
4th Street, NAC
Stoneleigh
Warwickshire CV8 2LG

Shetland Pony Stud Book
  Soc
Pedigree House
6 King's Place
Perth PH2 8AD

Shire Horse Soc
East of England
  Showground
Peterborough
Cambridgeshire PE2 6XE

Suffolk Horse Soc
The Market Hill
Woodbridge
Suffolk IP12 4LU

Welsh Part-Bred Horse
  Group
Bromsden Farm Stud
Henley on Thames
Oxon RG9 4RG

Welsh Pony and Cob Soc
6 Chalybeate Street
Aberystwyth
Dyfed SY23 1HS

AUSTRALIA

EFA – Federal Body
52 Kensington Road
Rose Park, SA 5067
Administration Only

EFA – NSW
GPO Box 4317
Sydney, NSW 2001
*Major event: NSW Horse
of the Year Show*

EFA – Queensland
PO Box 1417
Beenleigh, QLD 4207
*Major event: QLD Horse
of the Year Show*

EFA – Northern Territory
PO Box 1244
Palmerston, MT 0831
*Major event: Northern
Territory Horse of the Year
Show*

EFA – Victoria Royal
Showgrounds
Epsom Road
Ascot Vale, VIC 3032
*Major event: Victorian
Barastoc Horse of the Year
Show (Barastoc Stockfeeds
have been the sponsor of
this event for the past
twenty-five years, and the
event is better known as
'Barastoc' than as the
Victorian Horse of the Year
Show)*

EFA – South Australia
PO Box 1177
Marleston, SA 5033
*Major event: South
Australian Horse of the
Year Show*

EFA – Western Australia
PO Box 376
Midland, WA 6056
*Major event: Western
Australian Horse of the
Year Show*

EFA – Tasmania
PO Box 94
Glenorchy, TAS 7010
*Major event: Tasmanian
Horse of the Year Show*

The Hack Council of New
South Wales
PO Box 61
East Gosford 2250
*Major events: NSW Show
horse of the Year; The
Grand National Horse of
the Year Show*

The Hack Council of
Western Australia
9 Stevens Road
Bedfordale WA 6112

ROYAL SHOW SOCIETIES
NSW – Royal Agricultural
Soc of NSW
GPO Box 4317
Sydney, NSW 2001
*Major event: Sydney Royal
Easter Show – held over
each Easter weekend*

Queensland – Royal
National Agricultural &
Horticultural Assoc
Exhibitions Grounds
Gregory Terrace
Fortitude Valley, QLD 4005
*Major show: Royal
Brisbane Show – August*

South Australia – Royal
Agricultural &
Horticultural Soc of SA
PO Box 108
Goodwood, SA 5034
*Major show: Royal
Adelaide Show – September*

Tasmania – Royal
Agricultural Soc of
Tasmania
Royal Showgrounds
Glenorchy, TAS 7010
*Major show: Hobart Royal
– October*

Royal Launceston
Show Soc
PO Box 491
Launceston, TAS 7250
*Major show: Launceston –
October*

Victoria – Royal
Agricultural Soc of
Victoria
Royal Showgrounds
Epsom Road
Ascot Vale, VIC 3032
*Major show: Royal
Melbourne – September*

Western Australia – Royal
Agricultural Soc of WA
Royal Showgrounds
Claremont, WS 6010
*Major show: Royal Perth –
October*

Northern Territory – Royal
Australian Show Soc
PO Box 39600
Winellie, NT 0821
*Major show: Darwin and
Alice Springs – both held
in July*

USA

American Horse Shows
Assoc
220 E, 42nd Street
4th Floor
New York
NY 10017

American Horse Council
1700 K Street NW
Number 300
Washington
DC 20006

American Morgan Horse
Assoc
PO Box 960
3 Bostwick Road
Shelburne
VT 05482

American Quarter Horse
Assoc
2701 I–40 East
Amarillo
TX 79168

American Saddlebred
Horse Assoc
4093 Ironworks Pike
Lexington   KY 40511

Appaloosa Horse Club
PO Box 8304
Moscow
ID 83843

International Arabian
Horse Assoc
PO Box 33696
Denver
CO 80233

American Hackney Horse
Soc
4059 Iron Works Pike
Bldg A
Lexington
KY 40511

American Shetland Pony
Club
PO Box 3415
Peoria
IL 61612–3415

International Side-Saddle
Organization
PO Box 282
Alton Bay
NH 03810

National Show Horse
Registry
11700 Commonwealth
Drive
Suite 200
Louisville
KY 40299

Paso Fino Horse Assoc
PO Box 600
100 W Main Street
Bowling Green
FL 33834

Welsh Pony and Cob Soc
of America
PO Box 2977
Winchester
VA 22601

INDEX